A Taste of Freedom

A taste of freedom is printed for free distribution under the financial help of *'Phraya and Khunying Chavakij Banharn Fund'*

The Abbot, Wat Pah Nanachat, Bungwai, Warinchumrab, Ubolrajadhani 34110, Thailand

1 st. published - 1980	2,000 copies
2 nd. impression (revised) - 1982	5,000 copies
3 rd. impression - (revised) - 1991	5,000 copies

Production Manager : *Panita Angchandrpen*
Cover Design : *Panya Vijinthanasarn*
Cover's painting : **Double Miracle** by *Thanu Malakul Na Ayudhaya*

Contents

Acknowledgements

The production manager would like to thank *Venerable Ajahn Puriso,* the translator, who kindly not only revised the text for this edition, but also helped with the final proof-reading.

This book has come into existence with the help of many devoted people. *Khun Vanee Lamsam,* along with her brother *Khun Parl Na Pombejra,* raised the Fund to support all costs of publication. *Khun Thanu Malakul Na Ayudhaya* supplied us a slide of his beautiful painting for the cover. *Khun Panya Vijinthanasarn* helped with the cover design and illustrations. *Khun Chutima Thanapura* helped with the first proof-reading. *Khun Pansak Panpakdeedisakul* supplied us an invaluable photograph of Luang Por Chah (Phra Bodhinyāna Thera). *Khun Karoon Hansachainand* helped with the pasting some parts of the artwork and saw the book through the press. May the kind meritorious deeds of the above-mentioned people help them experience the supreme bliss, Nibbāna.

A Taste of Freedom

Introduction

The talks translated in this book were all taken from old cassette tape recordings of Venerable Ajahn Chah, some in Thai and some in the North-Eastern dialect, most recorded on poor quality equipment under less than optimum conditions. This presented some difficulty in the work of translation, which was overcome by occasionally omitting very unclear passages and at other times asking for advice from other listeners more familiar with those languages. Nevertheless there has inevitably been some editing in the process of making this book. Apart from the difficulties presented by the lack of clarity of the tapes, there is also the necessity of editing when one is taking words from the spoken to the written medium. For this, the translator takes full responsibility.

Pali words have occasionally been left as they are, in other cases translated. The criteria here has been readability. Those Pali words which were considered short enough or familiar enough to the reader already conversant with Buddhist terminology have generally been left untranslated. This should present no difficulty, as they are generally explained by the Venerable Ajahn in the course of the talk. Longer words, or words considered to be probably unfamiliar to the average reader, have been translated. Of these, there are two which are particularly noteworthy. They are *Kāmasukhallikānuyogo* and *Attakilamathānuyogo,* which have been translated as Indulgence in Pleasure and Indulgence in Pain respectively. These two words occur in no less than five of the talks included in this book, and although the translations provided here are not those generally used for these words, they are nevertheless in keeping with the Venerable Ajahn's use of them.

Venerable Ajahn Chah always gave his talks in simple, everyday language. His objective was to clarify the *Dhamma,* not to confuse his listeners with an overlog of information. Consequently the talks presented here have been rendered into correspondingly simple English. The aim has been to present Ajahn Chah's teaching in both the spirit and the letter.

In this third printing of **A Taste of Freedom,** a number of corrections have been made to clumsily worded passages, of which there are now hopefully less than in the first editions. For such inadequacies the translator must also take responsibility, and hopes the reader will bear with any literary shortcomings in order to receive the full benefit of the teachings contained herein.

The translator

About this mind...

About this mind... in truth there is nothing really wrong with it. It is intrinsically pure. Within itself it's already peaceful. That the mind is not peaceful these days is because it follows moods. The real mind doesn't have anything to it, it is simply (an aspect of) Nature. It becomes peaceful or agitated because moods deceive it. The untrained mind is stupid. Sense impressions come and trick it into happiness, suffering, gladness and sorrow, but the mind's true nature is none of those things. That gladness or sadness is not the mind, but only a mood coming to deceive us. The untrained mind gets lost and follows these things, it forgets itself. Then we think that it is we who are upset or at ease or whatever.

But really this mind of ours is already unmoving and peaceful ... really peaceful! Just like a leaf which is still as long as no wind blows. If a wind comes up the leaf flutters. The fluttering is due to the wind - the 'fluttering' is due to those sense impressions; the mind follows them. If it doesn't follow them, it doesn't 'flutter.'. If we know fully the true nature of sense impressions we will be unmoved.

Our practice is simply to see the Original Mind. So we must train the mind to know those sense impressions, and not get lost in them. To make it peaceful. Just this is the aim of all this difficult practice we put ourselves through.

"...That which 'looks over' the various factors which arise in meditation is 'sati', mindfulness. Sati is life. Whenever we don't have sati, when we are heedless, it's as if we are dead... This sati is simply presence of mind. It's a cause for the arising of self-awareness and wisdom ... Even when we are no longer in samādhi, sati should be present throughout..."

On meditation

To calm the mind means to find the right balance. If you try to fórce your mind too much it goes too far; if you don't try enough it doesn't get there, it misses the point of balance.

Normally the mind isn't still, it's moving all the time, it lacks strength. Making the mind strong and making the body strong are not the same. To make the body strong we have to exercise it, to push it, in order to make it strong, but to make the mind strong means to make it peaceful, not to go thinking of this and that. For most of us the mind has never been peaceful, it has never had the energy of *samādhi,** so we establish it within a boundary. We sit in meditation, staying with the *'one who knows'.*

If we force our breath to be too long or too short we're not balanced, the mind won't become peaceful. It's like when we first start to use a pedal sewing machine. At first we just practise pedalling the machine to get our co-ordination right, before we actually sew anything. Following the breath is similar. We don't get concerned over how long or short, weak or strong it is, we just note it. We simply let it be, following the natural breathing.

**Samādhi* is the state of concentrated calm resulting from meditation practice.

When it's balanced, we take the breathing as our meditation object. When we breathe in, the beginning of the breath is at the nose-tip, the middle of the breath at the chest and the end of the breath at the abdomen. This is the path of the breath. When we breathe out, the beginning of the breath is at the abdomen, the middle at the chest and the end at the nose-tip. We simply take note of this path of the breath at the nose-tip, the chest and the abdomen, then at the abdomen, the chest and the tip of the nose. We take note of these three points in order to make the mind firm, to limit mental activity so that mindfulness and self-awareness can easily arise.

When we are adept at noting these three points we can let them go and note the in and out breathing, concentrating solely at the nose-tip or the upper lip where the air passes on its in and out passage. We don't have to follow the breath, just to establish mindfulness in front of us at the nose-tip, and note the breath at this one point—entering, leaving, entering, leaving. There's no need to think of anything special, just concentrate on this simple task for now, having continuous presence of mind. There's nothing more to do, just breathing in and out.

Soon the mind becomes peaceful, the breath refined. The mind and body become light. This is the right state for the work of meditation.

When sitting in meditation the mind becomes refined, but whatever state it's in we should try to be aware of it, to know it. Mental activity is there together with tranquillity. There is *vitakka. Vitakka* is the action of bringing the mind to the theme of contemplation. If there is not much mindfulness, there will be not much *vitakka.* Then *vicāra,* the contemplation around that theme, follows. Various 'weak' mental impressions may arise from time to time but our self-awareness is the important thing—whatever may be happening we know it continuously. As we go deeper we are constantly aware of the state of our meditation, knowing whether or not the mind is firmly established. Thus, both concentration and awareness are present.

To have a peaceful mind does not mean that there's nothing happening, mental impressions do arise. For instance, when we talk about the first level of absorption, we say it has five factors. Along with *vitakka* and *vicāra, piti* (rapture) arises with the theme of contemplation and then *sukha* (happiness). These four things all lie together in the mind established in tranquillity. They are as one state.

The fifth factor is *ekaggatā* or one-pointedness. You may wonder how there can be one-pointedness when there are all these other factors as well. This is because they all become unified on that foundation of tranquillity. Together they are called a state of *samādhi.* They are not everyday states of mind, they are factors of absorption. There are these five characteristics, but they do not disturb the basic tranquillity. There is *vitakka,* but it does not disturb the mind; *vicāra,* rapture and happiness arise but do not disturb the mind. The mind is therefore as one with these factors. The first level of absorption is like this.

We don't have to call it First *Jhāna,* Second *Jhāna,* Third *Jhāna** and so on, let's just call it 'a peaceful mind'. As the mind becomes progressively calmer it will dispense with *vitakka* and *vicāra,* leaving only rapture and happiness. Why does the mind discard *vitakka* and *vicāra?* This is because, as the mind becomes more refined, the activity of *vitakka* and *vicāra* is too coarse to remain. At this stage, as the mind leaves off *vitakka* and *vicāra,* feelings of great rapture can arise, tears may gush out. But as the *samādhi* deepens rapture, too, is discarded, leaving only happiness and one-pointedness, until finally even happiness goes and the mind reaches its greatest refinement. There are only equanimity and one-pointedness, all else has been left behind. The mind stands unmoving

Once the mind is peaceful this can happen. You don't have to think a lot about it, it just happens by itself. This is called the energy of a peaceful mind. In this state the mind is not drowsy; the five hindrances, sense desire, aversion, restlessness, dullness and doubt, have all fled.

But if mental energy is still not strong and mindfulness weak, there will occasionally arise intruding mental impressoins. The mind is peaceful but it's as if there's a 'cloudiness' within the calm. It's not a normal sort

---

* *Jhāna* is an advanced state of concentration or *samādhi,* wherein the mind becomes absorbed into its meditation subject. It is divided into four levels, each level progressively more refined than the previous one.

of drowsiness though, some impressions will manifest – maybe we'll hear a sound or see a dog or something. It's not really clear but it's not a dream either. This is because these five factors have become unbalanced and weak.

The mind tends to play tricks within these levels of tranquillity. *'Imagery'* will sometimes arise when the mind is in this state, through any of the senses, and the meditator may not be able to tell exactly what is happening. "Am I sleeping? No. Is it a dream? No, it's not a dream..." These impressions arise from a middling sort of tranquillity; but if the mind is truly calm and clear we don't doubt the various mental impressions or imagery which arise. Questions like, "Did I drift off then? Was I sleeping? Did I get lost?..." don't arise, for they are characteristics of a mind which is still doubting. "Am I asleep or awake?"... Here, it's fuzzy! This is the mind getting lost in its moods. It's like the moon going behind a cloud. You can still see the moon but the clouds covering it render it hazy. It's not like the moon which has emerged from behind the clouds - clear, sharp and bright..

When the mind is peaceful and established firmly in mindfulness and self-awareness, there will be no doubt concerning the various phenomena which we encounter. The mind will truly be beyond the hindrances. We will clearly know as it is everything which arises in the mind. We do not doubt it because the mind is clear and bright. The mind which reaches *samādhi* is like this.

However some people find it hard to enter *samādhi* because it doesn't suit their tendencies. There is *samādhi,* but it's not strong or firm. But one can attain peace through the use of wisdom, through contemplating and seeing the truth of things, solving problems that way. This is using wisdom rather than the power of *samādhi.* To attain calm in practice it's not necessary to sit in meditation, for instance. Just ask yourself, "Ehh, what is that?..." and solve your problem right there! A person with wisdom is like this. Perhaps he can't really attain high levels of *samādhi,* although he develops some, enough to cultivate wisdom. It's like the difference between farming rice and farming corn. One can depend on rice more than corn for one's livelihood. Our practice can be like this, we depend more on wisdom to solve problems. When we see the truth, peace arises.

The two ways are not the same. Some people have insight and are strong in wisdom but do not have much *samādhi.* When they sit in meditation they aren't very peaceful. They tend to think a lot, contemplating this and that, until eventually they contemplate happiness and suffering and see the truth of them. Some incline more towards this than *samādhi.* Whether standing, walking, sitting or lying,* enlightenment of the Dhamma can take place. Through seeing, through relinquishing, they attain peace. They attain peace through knowing the truth without doubt, because they have seen it for themselves.

---

*That is, at all times, in all activities.

Other people have only little wisdom but their *samādhi* is very strong. They can enter very deep *samādhi* quickly, but not having much wisdom, they cannot catch their defilements, they don't know them. They can't solve their problems.

But regardless of whichever approach we use, we must do away with wrong thinking, leaving only Right View. We must get rid of confusion, leaving only peace. Either way we end up at the same place. There are these two sides to practice, but these two things, calm and insight, go together. We can't do away with either of them. They must go together.

That which 'looks over' the various factors which arise in meditation is *'sati'*, mindfulness. This *sati* is a condition which, through practice, can help other factors to arise. *Sati* is life. Whenever we don't have *sati,* when we are heedless, it's as if we are dead. If we have no sati, then our speech and actions have no meaning. This sati is simply recollection. It's a cause for the arising of self-awareness and wisdom. Whatever virtues we have cultivated are imperfect if lacking in *sati.* Sati is that which watches over us while standing, walking, sitting and lying. Even when we are no longer in *samādhi, sati* should be present throughout.

Whatever we do we take care. A sense of shame* will arise. We will feel ashamed about the things we do which aren't correct. As shame increases, our collected-

---

*This is a 'shame' based on knowledge of cause and effect, rather than mere emotional guilt.

ness will increase as well. When collectedness increases, heedlessness will disappear. Even if we don't sit in meditation, these factors will be present in the mind.

And this arises because of cultivating *sati*. Develop *sati!* This is the dhamma which looks over the work we are doing or have done in the past. It has real usefulness. We should know ourselves at all times. If we know ourselves like this, right will distinguish itself from wrong, the path will become clear, and cause for all shame will dissolve. Wisdom will arise.

We can bring the practice all together as morality, concentration and wisdom. To be collected, to be controlled, this is morality. The firm establishing of the mind within that control is concentration. Complete, overall knowledge within the activity in which we are engaged is wisdom. The practice in brief is just morality, concentration and wisdom, or in other words, the path. There is no other way.

"...With right samādhi, no matter what level of calm is reached, there is awareness. There is full mindfulness and clear comprehension. This is the samādhi which can give rise to wisdom, one cannot get lost in it. Practisers should understand this well..."

The path in harmony

Today I would like to ask you all. "Are you sure yet, are you certain in your meditation practice?" I ask because these days there are many people teaching meditation, both monks and laypeople, and I'm afraid you may be subject to wavering and doubt. If we understand clearly, we will be able to make the mind peaceful and firm.

You should understand *'the Eightfold Path'* as morality, concentration and wisdom. The path comes together as simply this. Our practice is to make this path arise within us.

When sitting meditation we are told to close the eyes, not to look at anything else, because now we are going to look directly at the mind. When we close our eyes, our attention comes inwards. We establish our attention on the breath, centre our feelings there, put our mindfulness there. When the factors of the path are in harmony we will be able to see the breath, the feelings, the mind and its moods for what they are. Here we will see the *'focus point'*, where *samādhi* and the other factors of the Path converge in harmony.

When we are sitting in meditation, following the breath, think to yourself that now you are sitting alone. There is no-one sitting around you, there is nothing at all. Develop this feeling that you are sitting alone until the mind lets go of all externals, concentrating solely on the breath. If you are thinking, "This person is sitting over here, that person is sitting over there," there is no peace, the mind doesn't come inwards. Just cast all that aside until you feel there is no-one sitting around you, until there is nothing at all, until you have no wavering or interest in your surroundings.

Let the breath go naturally, don't force it to be short or long or whatever, just sit and watch it going in and out. When the mind lets go of all external impressions, the sounds of cars and such will not disturb you. Nothing, whether sights or sounds, will disturb you, because the mind doesn't receive them. Your attention will come together on the breath.

If the mind is confused and won't concentrate on the breath, take a full, deep breath, as deep as you can, and then let it all out till there is none left. Do this three times and then re-establish your attention. The mind will become calm.

It's natural for it to be calm for a while, and then restlessness and confusion may arise again. When this happens, concentrate, breathe deeply again, and then re-establish your attention on the breath. Just keep going like this. When this has happened many times you will become adept at it, the mind will let go of all external manifestations. External impressions will not reach the mind. *Sati* will be firmly established. As the mind becomes more refined, so does the breath. Feelings will become finer and finer, the body and mind will be light. Our attention is solely on the inner, we see the in-breaths and out-breaths clearly, we see all impressions clearly. We will see the coming together of Morality, Concentration and Wisdom. This is called the Path in harmony. When there is this harmony our mind will be free of confusion, it will come together as one. This is called *samādhi.*

After watching the breath for a long time, it may become very refined; the awareness of the breath will gradually cease, leaving only bare awareness. The breath may become so refined it disappears! Perhaps we are *'just sitting'*, as if there is no breathing at all. Actually there is breathing, but it seems as if there's none. This is because the mind has reached its most refined state, there is just bare awareness. It has gone beyond the breath. The knowledge that the breath has disappeared becomes established. What will we take as our object of meditation now? We take just this knowledge as our object, that is, the awareness that there's no breath.

Unexpected things may happen at this time; some people experience them, some don't. If they do arise, we should be firm and have strong mindfulness. Some people see that the breath has disappeared and get a fright, they're afraid they might die. Here we should know the situation just as it is. We simply notice that there's no breath and take that as our object of awareness. This, we can say, is the firmest, surest type of *samādhi.* There is only one firm, unmoving state of mind. Perhaps the body will become so light it's as if there is no body at all. We feel like we're sitting in empty space, all seems empty. Although this may seem very unusual, you should understand that there's nothing to worry about. Firmly establish your mind like this.

When the mind is firmly unified, having no sense impressions to disturb it, one can remain in that state for any length of time. There will be no painful feelings to disturb us. When *samādhi* has reached this level, we can leave it when we choose, but if we come out of this *samādhi* we do so comfortably, not because we've become bored with it or tired. We come out because we've had enough for now, we feel at ease, we have no problems at all.

If we can develop this type of samādhi, then if we sit, say, thirty minutes or an hour, the mind will be cool and calm for many days. When the mind is cool and calm like this, it is clean. Whatever we experience, the mind will take up and investigate. This is a fruit of *samādhi.*

Morality has one function, concentration has another function and Wisdom another. These factors are like a cycle. We can see them all within the peaceful mind. When the mind is calm it has collectedness and restraint because of wisdom and the energy of concentration. As it becomes more collected it becomes more refined, which in turn gives morality the strength to increase in purity. As our morality becomes purer, this will help in the development of concentration. When concentration is firmly established it helps in the arising of wisdom. Morality, concentration and wisdom help each other, they are inter-related like this. In the end the Path becomes one and functions at all times. We should look after the strength which arises from the path, because it is the strength which leads to Insight and Wisdom.

On Dangers Of *Samādhi*

Samādhi is capable of bringing much harm or much benefit to the meditator, you can't say it brings only one or the other. For one who has no wisdom it is harmful, but for one who has wisdom it can bring real benefit, it can lead him to Insight.

That which can be most harmful to the meditator is Absorption *Samādhi (Jhāna)*, the *samādhi* with deep, sustained calm. This samādhi brings great peace. Where there is peace, there is happiness. When there is happiness, attachment and clinging to that happiness arise. The meditator doesn't want to contemplate anything else, he just wants to indulge in that pleasant feeling. When we have been practising for a long time we may become adept at entering this *samādhi* very quickly. As soon as we start to note our meditation object, the mind enters calm, and we don't want to come out to investigate anything. We just get stuck on that happiness. This is a danger to one who is practising meditation.

We must use *Upacāra Samādhi.* Here, we enter calm and then, when the mind is sufficiently calm, we come out and look at outer activity.* Looking at the outside with a calm mind gives rise to wisdom. This is hard to understand, because it's almost like ordinary thinking and imagining. When thinking is there, we may think the mind isn't peaceful, but actually that thinking is taking place within the calm. There is contemplation but it doesn't disturb the calm. We may bring thinking up in order to contemplate it. Here we take up the thinking to investigate it, it's not that we are aimlessly thinking or guessing away; it's something that arises from a peaceful mind. This is called *'awareness within calm and calm within awareness'.* If it's simply ordinary thinking and imagining, the mind won't be peaceful, it will be disturbed. But I am not talking about ordinary thinking, this is a feeling that arises from the peaceful mind. It's called *'contemplation'.* Wisdom is born right here.

So, there can be right *samādhi* and wrong *samādhi.* Wrong *samādhi* is where the mind enters calm and there's no awareness at all. One could sit for two hours

---

* 'Outer activity' refers to all manner of sense impressions. It is used in contrast to the 'inner inactivity' of absorption *samādhi (jhana),* where the mind does not 'go out' to external sense impressions.

or even all day but the mind doesn't know where it's been or what's happened. It doesn't know anything. There is calm, but that's all. It's like a well-sharpened knife which we don't bother to put to any use. This is a deluded type of calm, because there is not much self-awareness. The meditator may think he has reached the ultimate already, so he doesn't bother to look for anything else. *Samādhi* can be an enemy at this level. Wisdom cannot arise because there is no awareness of right and wrong.

With right *samādhi,* no matter what level of calm is reached, there is awareness. There is full mindfulness and clear comprehension. This is the *samādhi* which can give rise to wisdom, one cannot get lost in it. Practisers should understand this well. You can't do without this awareness, it must be present from beginning to end. This kind of *samādhi* has no danger.

You may wonder where does the benefit arise, how does the wisdom arise, from *samādhi?* When right *samādhi* has been developed, wisdom has the chance to arise at all times. When the eye sees form, the ear hears sound, the nose smells odour, the tongue experiences taste, the body experiences touch or the mind experiences mental impressions - in all postures - the mind stays with full knowledge of the true nature of those sense impressions, it doesn't follow them. When the mind has wisdom it doesn't *'pick and choose'.* In any posture we are fully aware of the birth of happiness and unhappiness. We let go of both of these things, we don't cling. This is called Right Practice, which is present in all postures. These words *'all postures'* do not refer only to bodily postures, they refer to the mind, which has mindfulness and clear comprehension of the truth at all times. When *samādhi* has been rightly developed, wisdom arises like this. This is called *'insight'*, knowledge of the truth.

There are two kinds of peace - the coarse and the refined. The peace which comes from *samādhi* is the coarse type. When the mind is peaceful there is happiness. The mind then takes this happiness to be peace. But happiness and unhappiness are becoming and birth. There is no escape from *samsāra** here because we still cling to them. So happiness is not peace, peace is not happiness.

The other type of peace is that which comes from wisdom. Here we don't confuse peace with happiness; we know the mind which contemplates and knows happiness and unhappiness as peace. The peace which arises from wisdom is not happiness, but is that which sees the truth of both happiness and unhappiness. Clinging to those states does not arise, the mind rises above them. This is the true goal of all Buddhist practice.

**Saṁsāra*, the wheel of Birth and Death, is the world of all conditioned phenomena, mental and material, which has the threefold characteristic of Impermanence, Unsatisfactoriness, and Not-self.

"...The Buddha laid down Morality, Concentration and Wisdom as the Path to peace, the way to enlightenment. But in truth these things are not the essence of Buddhism. They are merely the Path... The essence of Buddhism is peace, and that peace arises from truly knowing the nature of all things..."

The middle way within

The teaching of Buddhism is about giving up evil and practising good. Then, when evil is given up and goodness is established, we must let go of both good and evil. We have already heard enough about wholesome and unwholesome conditions to understand something about them, so I would like to talk about the Middle Way, that is, the path to escape from both of those things.

All the Dhamma talks and teachings of the Buddha have one aim - to show the way out of suffering to those who have not yet escaped. The teachings are for the purpose of giving us the right understanding. If we don't understand rightly, then we can't arrive at peace.

When the various Buddhas became enlightened and gave their first teachings, they all declared these two extremes - indulgence in pleasure and indulgence in pain.* These two ways are the ways of infatuation, they are the ways between which those who indulge in sense pleasures must fluctuate, never arriving at peace. They are the paths which spin around in *saṁsāra.*

---

*See Introduction.

The Enlightened One observed that all beings are stuck in these two extremes, never seeing the Middle Way of Dhamma, so he pointed them out in order to show the penalty involved in both. Because we are still stuck, because we are still wanting, we live repeatedly under theirs way. The Buddha declared that these two ways are the ways of intoxication, they are not the ways of a meditator, not the ways to peace. These ways are indulgence in pleasure and indulgence in pain, or, to put it simply, the way of slackness and the way of tension. If you investigate within, moment by moment, you will see that the tense way is anger, the way of sorrow. Going this way there is only difficulty and distress. Indulgence in Pleasure - if you've escaped from this, it means you've escaped from happiness. These ways, both happiness and unhappiness, are not peaceful states. The Buddha taught to let go of both of them. This is right practice. This is the Middle Way.

These words *'the Middle Way'* do not refer to our body and speech, they refer to the mind. When a mental impression which we don't like arises, it affects the mind and there is confusion. When the mind is confused, when it's *'shaken up'*, this is not the right way. When a mental impression arises which we like, the mind goes to indulgence in pleasure—that's not the way either.

We people don't want suffering, we want happiness. But in fact happiness is just a refined form of suffering. Suffering itself is the coarse form. You can compare them to a snake. The head of the snake is unhappiness, the tail of the snake is happiness. The head of the snake is really dangerous, it has the poisonous fangs. If you touch it, the snake will bite straight away, But never mind the head, even if you go and hold onto the tail, it will turn around and bite you just the same, because both the head and the tail belong to the one snake.

In the same way, both happiness and unhappiness, or pleasure and sadness, arise from the same parent — wanting. So when you're happy the mind isn't peaceful. It really isn't! For instance, when we get the things we like, such as wealth, prestige, praise or happiness, we become pleased as a result. But the mind still harbours some uneasiness because we're afraid of losing it. That very fear isn't a peaceful state. Later on we may actually lose that thing and then we really suffer. Thus, if you aren't aware, even if you're happy, suffering is imminent. It's just the same as grabbing the snake's tail - if you don't let go it will bite. So whether it's the snake's tail or its head, that is, wholesome or unwholesome conditions, they're all just characteristics of the Wheel of Existence, of endless change.

The Buddha established morality, concentration and wisdom as the path to peace, the way to enlightenment. But in truth these things are not the essence of Buddhism. They are merely the path. The Buddha called them *'Magga'*, which means 'path'. The essence of Buddhism is peace, and that peace arises from truly knowing the nature of all things. If we investigate closely, we can see that peace is neither happiness nor unhappiness. Neither of these is the truth.

The human mind, the mind which the Buddha exhorted us to know and investigate, is something we can only know by its activity. The true *'original mind'* has nothing to measure it by, there's nothing you can know it by. In its natural state it is unshaken, unmoving. When happiness arises all that happens is that this mind is getting lost in a mental impression, there is movement. When the mind moves like this, clinging and attachment to those things come into being.

The Buddha has already laid down the path of practice fully, but we have not yet practised, or if we have, we've practised only in speech. Our minds and our speech are not yet in harmony, we just indulge in empty talk. But the basis of Buddhism is not something that can be talked about or guessed at. The real basis of Buddhism is full knowledge of the truth of reality. If one knows this truth then no teaching is necessary. If one doesn't know, even if he listens to the teaching, he doesn't really hear. This is why the Buddha said, "The Enlightened One only points the way." He can't do the practice for you, because the truth is something you cannot put into words or give away.

All the teachings are merely similes and comparisons, means to help the mind see the truth. If we haven't seen the truth we must suffer. For example, we commonly say *'sankhāras'** when referring to the body. Anybody can say it, but in fact we have problems simply because we don't know the truth of these *sankhāras,* and thus cling to them. Because we don't know the truth of the body, we suffer.

Here is an example. Suppose one morning you're walking to work and a man yells abuse and insults at you from across the street. As soon as you hear this abuse your mind changes from its usual state. You don't feel so good, you feel angry and hurt. That man walks around abusing you night and day. When you hear the abuse, you get angry, and even when you return home you're still angry because you feel vindictive, you want to get even.

A few days later another man comes to your house and calls out, "Hey! That man who abused you the other day, he's mad, he's crazy! Has been for years! He abuses everybody like that. Nobody takes any notice of anything he says." As soon as you hear this you are suddenly relieved. That anger and hurt that you've pent up within you all these days melts away completely. Why? Because you know the truth of the matter now. Before, you didn't know, you thought that man was normal, so you were angry at him. Understanding like that caused you to suffer. As soon as you find out

*In the Thai language the word 'sungkahn', from the Pāli word *'sankhāra'* (the name given to all conditioned phenomena), is a commonly used term for the body. The Venerable Ajahn uses the word in both ways.

the truth, everything changes: "Oh, he's mad! That explains everything!" When you understand this you feel fine, because you know for yourself. Having known, then you can let go. If you don't know the truth you cling right there. When you thought that man who abused you was normal you could have killed him. But when you find out the truth, that he's mad, you feel much better. This is knowledge of the truth.

Someone who sees the Dhamma has a similar experience. When attachment, aversion and delusion disappear, they disappear in the same way. As long as we don't know these things we think, "What can I do? I have so much greed and aversion." This is not clear knowledge. It's just the same as when we thought the madman was sane. When we finally see that he was mad all along we're relieved of worry. No-one could show you this. Only when the mind sees for itself can it uproot and relinquish attachment.

It's the same with this body which we call *sankhāras.* Although the Buddha has already explained that it's not substantial or a real being as such, we still don't agree, we stubbornly cling to it. If the body could talk, it would be telling us all day long, "You're not my owner, you know." Actually it's telling us all the time, but it's Dhamma language, so we're unable to understand it. For instance, the sense organs of eye, ear, nose, tongue and body are continually changing, but I've never seen them ask permission from us even once! Like when we have a headache or a stomachache - the body never asks permission first, it just goes right ahead, following its natural course. This shows that the body doesn't allow anyone to be its owner, it doesn't have an owner. The Buddha described it as an empty thing.

We don't understand the Dhamma and so we don't understand these *sankhāras;* we take them to be ourselves, as belonging to us or belonging to others. This gives rise to clinging. When clinging arises, 'becoming' follows on. Once becoming arises, then there is birth. Once there is birth, then old age, sickness, death... the whole mass of suffering arises. This is the *Paticcasamuppāda**. We say ignorance gives rise to volitional activities, they give rise to consciousness and so on. All these things are simply events in mind. When we come into contact with something we don't like, if we don't have mindfulness, ignorance is there. Suffering arises straight away. But the mind passes through these changes so rapidly that we can't keep up with them. It's the same as when you fall from a tree. Before you know it - 'Thud!' - you've hit the ground. Actually you've passed many branches and twigs on the way but you couldn't count them, you couldn't remember them as you passed them. You just fall, and then 'Thud!'

The *Paticcasamuppāda* is the same as this. If we divide it up as it is in the scriptures, we say ignorance

---

**Paticcasamuppāda* — The Chain of Conditioned Arising, one of the central doctrines of Buddhist philosophy.

gives rise to volitional activities, volitional activities give rise to consciousness, consciousness gives rise to mind and matter, mind and matter give rise to the six sense bases, the sense bases give rise to sense contact, contact gives rise to feeling, feeling gives rise to wanting, wanting gives rise to clinging, clinging gives rise to becoming, becoming gives rise to birth, birth gives rise to old age, sickness, death, and all forms of sorrow. But in truth, when you come into contact with something you don't like, there's immediate suffering! That feeling of suffering is actually the result of the whole chain of the *Paticcasamuppāda*. This is why the Buddha exhorted his disciples to investigate and know fully their own minds.

When people are born into the world they are without names - once born, we name them. This is convention. We give people names for the sake of convenience, to call each other by. The scriptures are the same. We separate everything up with labels to make studying the reality convenient. In the same way, all things are simply *sankhāras*. Their original nature is merely that of things born of conditions. The Buddha said that they are impermanent, unsatisfactory and not-self. They are unstable. We don't understand this firmly, our understanding is not straight, and so we have wrong view. This wrong view is that the *sankhāras* are ourselves, we are the *sankhāras,* or that happiness and unhappiness are ourselves, we are happiness and unhappiness. Seeing like this is not full, clear knowledge of the true nature of things. The truth is that we can't force all these things to follow our desires, they follow the way of nature.

A simple comparison is this : suppose you go and sit in the middle of a freeway with the cars and trucks charging down at you. You can't get angry at the cars, shouting, "Don't drive over here! Don't drive over here!" It's a freeway, you can't tell them that! So what can you do? You get off the road! The road is the place where cars run, if you don't want the cars to be there, you suffer.

It's the same with *sankhāras.* We say they disturb us, like when we sit in meditation and hear a sound. We think, "Oh, that sound's bothering me." If we understand that the sound bothers us then we suffer accordingly. If we investigate a little deeper, we will see that it's we who go out and disturb the sound! The sound is simply sound. If we understand like this then there's nothing more to it, we leave it be. We see that the sound is one thing, we are another. One who understands that the sound comes to disturb him is one who doesn't see himself. He really doesn't! Once you see yourself, then you're at ease. The sound is just sound, why should you go and grab it? You see that actually it was you who went out and disturbed the sound. This is real knowledge of the truth. You see both sides, so you have peace. If you see only one side, there is suffering. Once you see both sides, then you follow the Middle Way. This is the right practice of the mind. This is what we call *'straightening out our understanding'*

In the same way, the nature of all *sankhāras* is impermanence and death, but we want to grab them, we carry them about and covet them. We want them to be true. We want to find truth within the things that aren't true! Whenever someone sees like this and clings to the *sankhāras* as being himself, he suffers. The Buddha wanted us to consider this.

The practice of Dhamma is not dependent on being a monk, a novice or a layman; it depends on straightening out your understanding. If our understanding is correct, we arrive at peace. Whether you are ordained or not it's the same, every person has the chance to practise Dhamma, to contemplate it. We all contemplate the same thing. If you attain peace, it's all the same peace; it's the same Path, with the same methods.

Therefore the Buddha didn't discriminate between laymen and monks, he taught all people to practise to know the truth of the *sankhāras.* When we know this truth, we let them go. If we know the truth there will be no more becoming or birth. How is there no more birth? There is no way for birth to take place because we fully know the truth of *sankhāras.* If we fully know the truth, then there is peace. Having or not having, it's all the same. Gain and loss are one. The Buddha taught us to know this. This is peace; peace from happiness, unhappiness, gladness and sorrow.

We must see that there is no reason to be born. Born in what way? Born into gladness: When we get something we like we are glad over it. If there is no clinging to that gladness there is no birth; if there is clinging, this is called *'birth'.* So if we get something, we aren't born (into gladness). If we lose, then we aren't born (into sorrow). This is the birthless and the deathless. Birth and death are both founded in clinging to and cherishing the sankhāras.

So the Buddha said. "There is no more becoming for me, finished is the holy life, this is my last birth." There! He knew the birthless and the deathless! This is what the Buddha constantly exhorted his disciples to know. This is the right practice. If you don't reach it, if you don't reach the Middle Way, then you won't transcend suffering.

"...Meditation means to make the mind peaceful in order to let wisdom arise... To put it shortly, it's just a matter of happiness and unhappiness. Happiness is pleasant feeling in the mind, unhappiness is just unpleasant feeling. The Buddha taught to separate this happiness and unhappiness from the mind..."

The peace beyond

It's of great importance that we practise the Dhamma. If we don't practise, then all our knowledge is only superficial knowledge, just the outer shell of it. It's as if we have some sort of fruit but we haven't eaten it yet. Even though we have that fruit in our hand we get no benefit from it. Only through the actual eating of the fruit will we really know its taste.

The Buddha didn't praise those who merely believe others, he praised the person who knows within himself. Just as with that fruit, if we have tasted it already, we don't have to ask anyone else if it's sweet or sour. Our problems are over. Why are they over? Because we see according to the truth. One who has realized the Dhamma is like one who has realized the sweetness or sourness of the fruit. All doubts are ended right here.

When we talk about Dhamma, although we may say a lot, it can usually be brought down to four things. They are simply to know suffering, to know the cause of suffering, to know the end of suffering and to know the path of practice leading to the end of suffering.

This is all there is. All that we have experienced on the path of practice so far comes down to these four things. When we know these things, our problems are over.

Where are these four things born? They are born just within the body and the mind, nowhere else. So why is the Dhamma of the Buddha so broad and expansive? This is so in order to explain these things in a more refined way, to help us to see them.

When Siddhattha Gotama was born into the world, before he saw the Dhamma, he was an ordinary person just like us. When he knew what he had to know, that is the truth of suffering, the cause, the end and the way leading to the end of suffering, he realized the Dhamma and became a perfectly Enlightened Buddha.

When we realize the Dhamma, wherever we sit we know Dhamma, wherever we are we hear the Buddha's teaching. When we understand Dhamma, the Buddha is within our mind, the Dhamma is within our mind, and the practice leading to wisdom is within our own mind. Having the Buddha, the Dhamma and the Saṅgha within our mind means that whether our actions are good or bad, we know clearly for ourselves their true nature. It was thus that the Buddha discarded worldly opinions, he discarded praise and criticism. When people praised or criticized him he just accepted it for what it was. These two things are simply worldly conditions so he wasn't shaken by them. Why not? Because he knew suffering. He knew that if he believed in that praise or criticism they would cause him to suffer.

When suffering arises it agitates us, we feel ill at ease. What is the cause of that suffering? It's because we don't know the Truth, this is the cause. When the cause is present, then suffering arises. Once arisen we don't know how to stop it. The more we try to stop it, the more it comes on. We say, "Don't criticize me," or "Don't blame me". Trying to stop it like this, suffering really comes on, it won't stop.

So the Buddha taught that the way leading to the end of suffering is to make the Dhamma arise as a reality within our own minds. We become one who witnesses the Dhamma for himself. If someone says we are good we don't get lost in it; they say we are no good and we don't forget ourselves. This way we can be free. *'Good'* and *'evil'* are just worldly dhammas, they are just states of mind. If we follow them our mind becomes the world, we just grope in the darkness and don't know the way out. If it's like this then we have not yet mastered ourselves. We try to defeat others, but in doing so we only defeat ourselves; but if we have mastery over ourselves then we have mastery over all - over all mental formations, sights, sounds, smells, tastes and bodily feelings.

Now I'm talking about externals, they're like that, but the outside is reflected inside also. Some people only know the outside, they don't know the inside. Like when we say to *'see the body in the body'*. Having seen the outer body is not enough, we must know the body within the body. Then, having investigated the mind, we should know the mind within the mind.

Why should we investigate the body? What is this *'body in the body'?* When we say to know the mind, what is this *'mind'?* If we don't know the mind then we don't know the things within the mind. This is to be someone who doesn't know suffering, doesn't know the cause, doesn't know the end and doesn't know the way. The things which should help to extinguish suffering don't help, because we get distracted by the things which aggravate it. It's just as if we have an itch on our head and we scratch our leg! If it's our head that's itchy then we're obviously not going to get much relief. In the same way, when suffering arises we don't know how to handle it, we don't know the practice leading to the end of suffering.

For instance, take this body, this body that each of us has brought along to this meeting. If we just see the form of the body there's no way we can escape suffering. Why not? Because we still don't see the inside of the body, we only see the outside. We only see it as something beautiful, something substantial. The Buddha said that only this is not enough. We see the outside with our eyes; a child can see it, animals can see it, it's not difficult. The outside of the body is easily seen, but having seen it we stick to it, we don't know the truth of it. Having seen it we grab onto it and it bites us!

So we should investigate the body within the body. Whatever's in the body, go ahead and look at it. If we just see the outside it's not clear. We see hair, nails and so on and they are just pretty things which entice us, so the Buddha taught to see the inside of the body, to see the body within the body. What is in the body? Look closely within! We will see many things inside to surprise us, because even though they are within us, we've never seen them. Wherever we walk we carry them with us, sitting in a car we carry them with us, but we still don't know them at all!

It's as if we visit some relatives at their house and they give us a present. We take it and put it in our bag and then leave without opening it to see what is inside. When at last we open it - full of poisonous snakes! Our body is like this. If we just see the shell of it we say it's fine and beautiful. We forget ourselves. We forget impermanence, unsatisfactoriness and not-self. If we look within this body it's really repulsive. If we look according to reality, without trying to sugar things over, we'll see that it's really pitiful and wearisome. Dispassion will arise. This feeling of *'disinterest'* is not that we feel aversion for the world or anything; it's simply our mind clearing up, our mind letting go. We see things as not substantial or dependable, but that all things are naturally established just as they are. However we want them to be, they just go their own way regardless. Whether we laugh or cry, they simply are the way they are. Things which are unstable are unstable; things which are not beautiful are not beautiful.

So the Buddha said that when we experience sights, sounds, tastes, smells, bodily feelings or mental states, we should release them. When the ear hears sounds, let them go. When the nose smells an odour, let it go... just leave it at the nose! When bodily feelings arise, let go of the like or dislike that follow, let them go back to their birth-place. The same for mental states. All these things, just let them go their way. This is knowing. Whether it's happiness or unhappiness, it's all the same. This is called meditation.

Meditation means to make the mind peaceful in order to let wisdom arise. This requires that we practise with body and mind in order to see and know the sense impressions of form, sound, taste, smell, touch and mental formations. To put it shortly, it's just a matter of happiness and unhappiness. Happiness is pleasant feeling in the mind, unhappiness is just unpleasant feeling. The Buddha taught to separate this happiness and unhappiness from the mind. The mind is that which knows. Feeling* is the characteristic of happiness or unhappiness, like or dislike. When the mind indulges in these things we say that it clings to or takes that happiness and unhappiness to be worthy of holding. That clinging is an action of mind, that happiness or unhappiness is feeling.

---

*Feeling is a translation of the Pāli word *'Vedanā'*, and should be understood in the sense Ajahn Chah herein describes it: as the mental states of like, dislike, gladness, sorrow etc.

When we say the Buddha told us to separate the mind from the feeling, he didn't literally mean to throw them to different places. He meant that the mind must know happiness and know unhappiness. When sitting in *samādhi,* for example, and peace fills the mind, then happiness comes but it doesn't reach us, unhappiness comes but doesn't reach us. This is to separate the feeling from the mind. We can compare it to oil and water in a bottle. They don't combine. Even if you try to mix them, the oil remains oil and the water remains water. Why is this so? Because they are of different density.

The natural state of the mind is neither happiness nor unhappiness. When feeling enters the mind then happiness or unhappiness is born. If we have mindfulness then we know pleasant feeling as pleasant feeling. The mind which knows will not pick it up. Happiness is there but it's *'outside'* the mind, not buried within the mind. The mind simply knows it clearly.

If we separate unhappiness from the mind, does that mean there is no suffering, that we don't experience it? Yes, we experience it, but we know mind as mind, feeling as feeling. We don't cling to that feeling or carry it around. The Buddha separated these things through knowledge. Did he have suffering? He knew the state of suffering but he didn't cling to it, so we say that he cut suffering off. And there was happiness too, but he knew that happiness, if it's not known, is like a poison. He didn't hold it to be himself. Happiness was there through knowledge, but it didn't exist in his mind. Thus we say that he separated happiness and unhappiness from his mind.

When we say that the Buddha and the Enlightened Ones killed defilements,* it's not that they really killed them. If they had killed all defilements then we probably wouldn't have any! They didn't kill defilements; when they knew them for what they are, they let them go. Someone who's stupid will grab them, but the Enlightened Ones knew the defilements in their own minds as a poison, so they swept them out. They swept out the things which caused them to suffer, they didn't kill them. One who doesn't know this will see some things, such as happiness, as good, and then grab them, but the Buddha just knew them and simply brushed them away.

But when feeling arises for us we indulge in it, that is, the mind carries that happiness and unhappiness around. In fact they are two different things. The activities of mind, pleasant feeling, unpleasant feeling and so on, are mental impressions, they are the world. If the mind knows this it can equally do work involving happiness or unhappiness. Why? Because it knows the truth of these things. Someone who doesn't know them sees them as having different value, but one who knows sees them as equal. If you cling to happiness it will be the birth-place of unhappiness later on, because

---

*Defilements, or *'Kilesa'*, are the habits born of Ignorance which infest the minds of all unenlightened beings.

happiness is unstable, it changes all the time. When happiness disappears, unhappiness arises.

The Buddha knew that because both happiness and unhappiness are unsatisfactory, they have the same value. When happiness arose he let it go. He had right practice, seeing that both these things have equal values and drawbacks. They come under the Law of Dhamma, that is, they are unstable and unsatisfactory. Once born, they die. When he saw this, right view arose, the right way of practice became clear. No matter what sort of feeling or thinking arose in his mind, he knew it as simply the continuous play of happiness and unhappiness. He didn't cling to them.

When the Buddha was newly enlightened he gave a sermon about Indulgence in Pleasure and Indulgence in Pain. "Monks! Indulgence in Pleasure is the loose way, Indulgence in Pain is the tense way." These were the two things that disturbed his practice until the day he was enlightened, because at first he didn't let go of them. When he knew them, he let them go, and so was able to give his first sermon.

So we say that a meditator should not walk the way of happiness or unhappiness, rather he should know them. Knowing the truth of suffering, he will know the cause of suffering, the end of suffering and the way leading to the end of suffering. And the way out of suffering is meditation itself. To put it simply, we must be mindful.

Mindfulness is knowing, or presence of mind. Right now what are we thinking, what are we doing? What do we have with us right now? We observe like this, we are aware of how we are living. When we practise like this wisdom can arise. We consider and investigate at all times, in all postures. When a mental impression arises that we like we know it as such, we don't hold it to be anything substantial. It's just happiness. When unhappiness arises we know that it's Indulgence in Pain, it's not the path of a meditator.

This is what we call separating the mind from the feeling. If we are clever we don't attach, we leave things be. We become the *'one who knows'*. The mind and feeling are just like oil and water; they are in the same bottle but they don't mix. Even if we are sick or in pain, we still know the feeling as feeling, the mind as mind. We know the painful or comfortable states but we don't identify with them. We stay only with peace: the peace beyond both comfort and pain.

You should understand it like this, because if there is no permanent self then there is no refuge. You must live like this, that is, without happiness and without unhappiness. You stay only with the knowing, you don't carry things around.

As long as we are still unenlightened all this may sound strange but it doesn't matter, we just set our goal in this direction. The mind is the mind. It meets happiness and unhappiness and we see them as merely that, there's nothing more to it. They are divided, not mixed. If they are all mixed up then we don't know them. It's like living in a house; the house and its occupant are related, but separate. If there is danger in our house we are distressed because we must protect it, but if the house catches fire we get out of it. If painful feeling arises we get out of it, just like that house. When it's full of fire and we know it, we come running out of it. They are separate things; the house is one thing, the occupant is the other.

We say that we separate mind and feeling in this way but in fact they are by nature already separate. Our realization is simply to know this natural separateness according to reality. When we say they are not separated it's because we're clinging to them through ignorance of the truth.

So the Buddha told us to meditate. This practice of meditation is very important. Merely to know with the intellect is not enough. The knowledge which arises from practice with a peaceful mind and the knowledge which comes from study are really far apart. The knowledge which comes from study is not real knowledge of our mind. The mind tries to hold onto and keep this knowledge. Why do we try to keep it? Just to lose it! And then when it's lost we cry!

If we really know, then there's letting go, leaving things be. We know how things are and don't forget ourselves. If it happens that we are sick we don't get lost in that. Some people think, "This year I was sick the whole time, I couldn't meditate at all." These are the words of a really foolish person. Someone who's sick or dying should really be diligent in his practice. One may say he doesn't have time to meditate. He's sick, he's suffering, he doesn't trust his body, and so he feels that he can't meditate. If we think like this then things are difficult. The Buddha didn't teach like that. He said that right here is the place to meditate. When we're sick or almost dying that's when we can really know and see reality.

Other people say they don't have the chance to meditate because they're too busy. Sometimes school teachers come to see me. They say they have many responsibilities so there's no time to meditate. I ask them, "When you're teaching do you have time to breathe?" They answer, "Yes." "So how can you have time to breathe if the work is so hectic and confusing? Here you are far from Dhamma."

Actually this practice is just about the mind and its feelings. It's not something that you have to run after or struggle for. Breathing continues while working. Nature takes care of the natural processes - all we have to do is try to be aware. Just to keep trying, going inwards to see clearly. Meditation is like this.

If we have that presence of mind then whatever work we do will be the very tool which enables us to know right and wrong continually. There's plenty of time to meditate, we just don't fully understand the practice, that's all. While sleeping we breathe, eating we breathe, don't we? Why don't we have time to meditate? Wherever we are we breathe. If we think like this then our life has as much value as our breath, wherever we are we have time.

All kinds of thinking are mental conditions, not conditions of body, so we need simply have presence of mind, then we will know right and wrong at all times. Standing, walking, sitting and lying, there's plenty of time. We just don't know how to use it properly. Please consider this.

We cannot run away from feeling, we must know it. Feeling is just feeling, happiness is just happiness, unhappiness is just unhappiness. They are simply that. So why should we cling to them? If the mind is clever, simply to hear this is enough to enable us to separate feeling from the mind.

If we investigate like this continuously the mind will find release, but it's not escaping through ignorance. The mind lets go, but it knows. It doesn't let go through stupidity, not because it doesn't want things to be the way they are. It lets go because it knows according to the truth. This is seeing nature, the reality that's all around us.

When we know this we are someone who's skilled with the mind, we are skilled with mental impressions. When we are skilled with mental impressions we are skilled with the world. This is to be a *'Knower of the World.'* The Buddha was someone who clearly knew the world with all its difficulty. He knew the troublesome, and that which was not troublesome was right there. This world is so confusing, how is it that the Buddha was able to know it? Here we should understand that the Dhamma taught by the Buddha is not beyond our ability. In all postures we should have presence of mind and self awareness - and when it's time to sit meditation we do that.

We sit in meditation to establish peacefulness and cultivate mental energy. We don't do it in order to play around at anything special. Insight meditation is sitting in *samādhi* itself. At some places they say, "Now we are going to sit in *samādhi,* after that we'll do insight meditation." Don't divide them like this! Tranquillity is the base which gives rise to wisdom; wisdom is the fruit of tranquillity. To say that now we are going to do calm meditation, later we'll do insight - you can't do that! You can only divide them in speech. Just like a knife, the blade is on one side, the back of the blade on the other. You can't divide them. If you pick up one side you get both sides. Tranquillity gives rise to wisdom like this.

Morality is the father and mother of Dhamma. In the beginning we must have morality. Morality is peace. This means that there are no wrong doings in body or speech. When we don't do wrong then we don't get agitated; when we don't become agitated then peace and collectedness arise within the mind. So we say that morality, concentration and wisdom are the path on which all the Noble Ones have walked to enlightenment. They are all one. Morality is concentration, concentration is morality. Concentration is wisdom, wisdom is concentration. It's like a mango. When it's a flower we call it a flower. When it becomes a fruit we call it a mango. When it ripens we call it a ripe mango. It's all one mango but it continually changes. The big mango grows from the small mango, the small mango becomes a big one. You can call them different fruits or all one. Morality, concentration and wisdom are related like this. In the end it's all the path that leads to enlightenment.

The mango, from the moment it first appears as a flower, simply grows to ripeness. This is enough, we should see it like this. Whatever others call it, it doesn't matter Once it's born it grows to old age, and then where? We should contemplate this.

Some people don't want to be old. When they get old they become regretful. These people shouldn't eat ripe mangoes! Why do we want the mangoes to be ripe? If they're not ripe in time,, we ripen them artificially, don't we? But when we become old we are filled with regret. Some people cry, they're afraid to get old or die. If it's like this then they shouldn't eat ripe mangoes, better eat just the flowers! If we can see this then we can see the Dhamma. Everything clears up, we are at peace. Just determine to practise like that.

So today the Chief Privy Councillor and his party have come together to hear the Dhamma. You should take what I've said and contemplate it. If anything is not right, please excuse me. But for you to know whether it's right or wrong depends on your practising and seeing for yourselves. Whatever's wrong, throw it out. If it's right then take it and use it. But actually we practise in order to let go of both right and wrong. In the end we just throw everything out. If it's right, throw it out; wrong, throw it out! Usually if it's right we cling to rightness, if it's wrong we hold it to be wrong, and then arguments follow. But the Dhamma is the place where there's nothing - nothing at all.

"...The Buddha was enlightened in the world, he contemplated the world. If he hadn't contemplated the world, if he hadn't seen the world, he couldn't have risen above it. The Buddha's enlightenment was simply enlightenment of this very world. The world was still there: gain and loss, praise and criticism, fame and disrepute, happiness and unhappiness were all still there. If there weren't these things there would be nothing to become enlightened to..."

Opening the Dhamma eye

Some of us start to practise, and even after a year or two, still don't know what's what. We are still unsure of the practice. When we're still unsure, we don't see that everything around us is purely Dhamma, and so we turn to teachings from the Ajahns. But actually, when we know our own mind, when there is *sati* to look closely at the mind, there is wisdom. All times and all places become occasions for us to hear the Dhamma.

We can learn Dhamma from nature, from trees for example. A tree is born due to causes and it grows following the course of nature. Right here the tree is teaching us Dhamma, but we don't understand this. In due course, it grows and grows until it buds, flowers and fruit appear. All we see is the appearance of the flowers and fruit; we're unable to bring this within and contemplate it. Thus we don't know that the tree is teaching us Dhamma. The fruit appears and we merely eat it without investigating: sweet, sour or salty, it's the nature of the fruit. And this is Dhamma, the teaching of the fruit. Following on, the leaves grow old. They wither, die and then fall from the tree. All we see is that the leaves have fallen down. We step on them, we sweep them up, that's all. We don't investigate thoroughly, so we don't know that nature is teaching us. Later on the new leaves sprout, and we merely see that, without taking it further. We don't bring these things into our minds to contemplate.

If we can bring all this inwards and investigate it, we will see that the birth of a tree and our own birth are no different. This body of ours is born and exists dependent on conditions, on the elements of earth, water, wind and fire. It has its food, it grows and grows. Every part of the body changes and flows according to its nature. It's no different from the tree; hair, nails, teeth and skin - all change. If we know the things of nature, then we will know ourselves.

People are born. In the end they die. Having died they are born again. Nails, teeth and skin are constantly dying and re-growing. If we understand the practice then we can see that a tree is no different from ourselves. If we understand the teaching of the Ajahns, then we realize that the outside and the inside are comparable. Things which have consciousness and those without consciousness do not differ. They are the same. And if we understand this sameness, then when we see the nature of a tree, for example, we will know that it's no different from our own five *'khandhas'** - body, feeling, memory, thinking and consciousness. If we have this understanding then we understand Dhamma. If we understand

* 'Khandhas'. They are the five 'groups' which go to make up what we call 'a person'.

Dhamma we understand the five *'khandhas'*, how they constantly shift and change, never stopping.

So whether standing, walking, sitting or lying we should have *sati* to watch over and look after the mind. When we see external things it's like seeing internals. When we see internals it's the same as seeing externals. If we understand this then we can hear the teaching of the Buddha. If we understand this, then we can say that Buddha-nature, the *'one who knows'*, has been established. It knows the external. It knows the internal. It understands all things which arise. Understanding like this, then sitting at the foot of a tree we hear the Buddha's teaching. Standing, walking, sitting or lying, we hear the Buddha's teaching. Seeing, hearing, smelling, tasting, touching and thinking, we hear the Buddha's teaching. The Buddha is just this *'One who knows'* within this very mind. It knows the Dhamma, it investigates the Dhamma. It's not that the Buddha who lived so long ago comes to talk to us, but this Buddha-nature, the *'One who knows'*, arises. The mind becomes illumined.

If we establish the Buddha within our mind then we see everything, we contemplate everything, as no different from ourselves. We see various animals, trees, mountains and vines as no different from ourselves. We see poor people and rich people - they're no different from us. Black people and white people - no different! They all have the same characteristics. One who understands like this is content wherever he is. He listens to the Buddha's teaching at all times. If we don't understand this, then even if we spend all our time listening to teachings from the various Ajahns, we still won't understand their meaning.

The Buddha said that enlightenment of the Dhamma is just knowing Nature*, the reality which is all around us, the Nature which is right here! If we don't understand this Nature we experience disappointment and joy, we get lost in moods, giving rise to sorrow and regret. Getting lost in mental objects is getting lost in Nature. When we get lost in Nature then we don't know Dhamma. The Enlightened One merely pointed out this Nature.

Having arisen, all things change and die. Things we make, such as plates, bowls and dishes, all have the same characteristic. A bowl is molded into being due to a cause, man's impulse to create, and as we use it, it gets old, breaks up and disappears. Trees, mountains and vines are the same, right up to animals and people.

When *Aññā Kondañña,* the first disciple, heard the Buddha's teaching for the first time, the realization he had was nothing very complicated. He simply saw that whatever thing is born, that thing must change and grow old as a natural condition and eventually it must die. *Aññā Kondañña* had never thought of this before, or if he had it wasn't thoroughly clear, so he hadn't yet let go, he still clung to the *khandhas.* As he sat mindfully listening to the Buddha's discourse, Buddha-nature arose

---

* Nature here refers to all things, mental and physical, not just trees, animals etc.

in him. He received a sort of Dhamma 'transmission', which was the knowledge that all conditioned things are impermanent. Any thing which is born must have ageing and death as a natural result.

This feeling was different from anything he'd ever known before. He truly realized his mind, and so 'Buddha' arose within him. At that time the Buddha declared that *Aññā Kondañña* had received the Eye of Dhamma.

What is it that this Eye of Dhamma sees? This Eye sees that whatever is born has ageing and death as a natural result. *'Whatever is born'* means everything! Whether material or immaterial, it all comes under this *'whatever is born'*. It refers to all of Nature. Like this body for instance - it's born and then proceeds to extinction. When it's small it *'dies'* from smallness to youth. After a while it *'dies'* from youth and becomes middle-aged. Then it goes on to 'die' from middle-age and reach old-age, finally reaching the end. Trees, mountains and vines all have this characteristic.

So the vision or understanding of the *'One who knows'* clearly entered the mind of *Aññā Kondañña* as he sat there. This knowledge of *'whatever is born'* became deeply embedded in his mind, enabling him to uproot attachment to the body. This attachment was *'sakkāyaditthi'*. This means that he didn't take the body to be a self or a being, or in terms of 'he' or 'me'. He didn't cling to it. He saw it clearly, thus uprooting *sakkāyaditthi*.

And the *vicikicchā* (doubt) was destroyed. Having uprooted attachment to the body he didn't doubt his realization. *Sīlabbata parāmāsa** was also uprooted. His practice became firm and straight. Even if his body was in pain or fever he didn't grasp it, he didn't doubt. He didn't doubt, because he had uprooted clinging. This grasping of the body is called *sīlabbata parāmāsa.* When one uproots the view of the body being the self, grasping and doubt are finished with. If just this view of the body as the self arises within the mind then grasping and doubt begin right there.

So as the Buddha expounded the Dhamma, *Aññā Kondañña* opened the Eye of Dhamma. This Eye is just the *'One who knows* clearly'. It sees things differently. It sees this very Nature. Seeing Nature clearly, clinging is uprooted and the *'One who knows'* is born. Previously he knew but he still had clinging. You could say that he knew the Dhamma but he still hadn't *seen* it, or he had seen the Dhamma but still wasn't one with it.

At this time the Buddha said, "*Kondañña* knows." What did he know? He just knew Nature! Usually we get lost in Nature, as with this body of ours. Earth,

---

* *Sīlabbata parāmāsa* is traditionally translated as attachment to rites and rituals. Here the Venerable Ajahn relates it, along with doubt, specifically to the body. These three things, *Sakkāyaditthi, Vicikicchā,* and *Sīlabbata parāmāsa,* are, in the scriptures, the first three of ten *'fetters'*, which are given up on the first glimpse of Enlightenment, known as *'Stream Entry'.* At full Enlightenment all ten *'fetters'* are transcended.

water, fire and wind come together to make this body. It's an aspect of Nature, a material object we can see with the eye. It exists depending on food, growing and changing until finally it reaches extinction.

Coming inwards, that which watches over the body is consciousness - just this *'one who knows'*, this single awareness. If it receives through the eye it's called seeing. If it receives through the ear it's called hearing; through the nose it's called smelling; through the tongue, tasting; through the body, touching; and through the mind, thinking. This consciousness is just one but when it functions at different places we call it different things. Through the eye we call it one thing, through the ear we call it another. But whether it functions at the eye, ear, nose, tongue, body or mind it's just one awareness. Following the scriptures we call it the six consciousnesses, but in reality there is only one consciousness arising at these six different bases. There are six 'doors' but a single awareness, which is this very mind.

This mind is capable of knowing the truth of Nature. If the mind still has obstructions, then we say it knows through Ignorance. It knows wrongly and it sees wrongly. Knowing wrongly and seeing wrongly, or knowing and seeing rightly, it's just a single awareness. We say wrong view and right view but it's just one thing. Right and wrong both arise from this one place. When there is wrong knowledge we say that Ignorance conceals the truth. When there is wrong knowledge then there is wrong view, wrong intention, wrong action, wrong livelihood - everything is wrong! And on the other hand the path of right practice is born in this same place. When there is right then the wrong disappears.

The Buddha practised enduring many hardships and torturing himself with fasting and so on, but he investigated deeply into his mind until finally he uprooted ignorance. All the Buddhas were enlightened in mind, because the body knows nothing. You can let it eat or not, it doesn't matter, it can die at any time. The Buddhas all practised with the mind. They were enlightened in mind.

The Buddha, having contemplated his mind, gave up the two extremes of practice - indulgence in pleasure and indulgence in pain - and in his first discourse expounded the Middle Way between these two. But we hear his teaching and it grates against our desires. We're infatuated with pleasure and comfort, infatuated with happiness, thinking we are good, we are fine - this is indulgence in pleasure. It's not the right path. Dissatisfaction, displeasure, dislike and anger - this is indulgence in pain. These are the extreme ways which one on the path of practice should avoid.

These *'ways'* are simply the happiness and unhappiness which arise. The 'one on the path' is this very mind, the 'one who knows'. If a good mood arises we cling to it as good, this is indulgence in pleasure. If an unpleasant mood arises we cling to it through dislike - this is indulgence in pain. These are the wrong paths, they aren't the ways of a meditator. They're the ways of the worldly, those who look for fun and happiness and shun unpleasantness and suffering.

The wise know the wrong paths but they relinquish them, they give them up. They are unmoved by pleasure and displeasure, happiness and unhappiness. These things arise but those who know don't cling to them, they let them go according to their nature. This is right view. When one knows this fully there is liberation. Happiness and unhappiness have no meaning for an Enlightened One.

The Buddha said that the Enlightened Ones were far from defilements. This doesn't mean that they ran away from defilements, they didn't run away anywhere. Defilements were there. He compared it to a lotus leaf in a pond of water. The leaf and the water exist together, they are in contact, but the leaf doesn't become damp. The water is like defilements and the lotus leaf is the Enlightened Mind.

The mind of one who practises is the same; it doesn't run away anywhere, it stays right there. Good, evil, happiness and unhappiness, right and wrong arise, and he knows them all. The meditator simply knows them, they don't enter his mind. That is, he has no clinging. He is simply the experiencer. To say he simply experiences is our common language. In the language of Dhamma we say he lets his mind follow the Middle Way.

These activities of happiness, unhappiness and so on are constantly arising because they are characteristics of the world. The Buddha was enlightened in the world, he contemplated the world. If he hadn't contemplated the world, if he hadn't seen the world, he couldn't have risen above it. The Buddha's Enlightenment was simply enlightenment of this very world. The world was still there: gain and loss, praise and criticism, fame and disrepute, happiness and unhappiness were all still there. If there weren't these things there would be nothing to become enlightened to! What he knew was just the world, that which surrounds the hearts of people. If people follow these things, seeking praise and fame, gain and happiness, and trying to avoid their opposites, they sink under the weight of the world.

Gain and loss, praise and criticism, fame and disrepute, happiness and unhappiness - this is the world. The person who is lost in the world has no path of escape, the world overwhelms him. This world follows the Law of Dhamma so we call it worldly dhamma. He who lives within the worldly dhamma is called a worldly being. He lives surrounded by confusion.

Therefore the Buddha taught us to develop the path. We can divide it up into morality, concentration and wisdom - develop them to completion! This is the path of practice which destroys the world. Where is this world? It is just in the minds of beings infatuated with it! The action of clinging to praise, gain, fame, happiness and unhappiness is called *'world'*. When it is there in the mind, then the world arises, the worldly being is born. The world is born because of desire. Desire is the birthplace of all worlds. To put an end to desire is to put an end to the world.

Our practice of morality, concentration and wisdom is otherwise called the Eightfold Path. This Eightfold Path and the eight worldly dhammas are a pair. How is it that they are a pair? If we speak according to the scriptures, we say that gain and loss, praise and criticism, fame and disrepute, happiness and unhappiness are the eight worldly dhammas. Right View, Right Intention, Right Speech, Right Action, Right Livelihood, Right Effort, Right mindfulness and Right concentration, this is the Eightfold Path. These two eightfold ways exist in the same place. The eight worldly dhammas are right here in this very mind, with the 'one who knows'; but this *'one who knows'* has obstructions, so it knows wrongly and thus becomes the world. It's just this one *'one who knows'*, no other! The Buddha-nature has not yet arisen in this mind, it has not yet extracted itself from the world. The mind like this is the world.

When we practise the path, when we train our body and speech, it's all done in that very same mind. It's in the same place so they see each other; the path sees the world. If we practise with this mind of ours we encounter this clinging to praise, fame, pleasure and happiness, we see the attachment to the world.

The Buddha said, "You should know the world. It dazzles like a king's royal carriage. Fools are entranced, but the wise are not deceived." It's not that he wanted us to go all over the world looking at everything, studying everything about it. He simply wanted us to watch this mind which is attached to it. When the Buddha told us to look at the world he didn't want us to get stuck in it, he wanted us to investigate it, because the world is born just in this mind. Sitting in the shade of a tree you can look at the world. When there is desire the world comes into being right there. Wanting is the birth place of the world. To extinguish wanting is to extinguish the world.

When we sit in meditation we want the mind to become peaceful, but it's not peaceful. Why is this? We don't want to think but we think. It's like a person who goes to sit on an ants' nest: the ants just keep on biting him. When the mind is the world then even sitting still with our eyes closed, all we see is the world. Pleasure, sorrow, anxiety, confusion - it all arises. Why is this? It's because we still haven't realized Dhamma. If the mind is like this the meditator can't endure the worldly dhammas, he doesn't investigate. It's just the same as if he were sitting on an ants' nest. The ants are going to bite because he's right on their home! So what should he do? He should look for some poison or use fire to drive them out.

But most Dhamma practisers don't see it like that. If they feel content they just follow contentment, feeling discontent they just follow that. Following the worldly dhammas the mind becomes the world. Sometimes we may think, "Oh, I can't do it, it's beyond me," ... so we don't even try! This is because the mind is full of defilements, the worldly dhammas prevent the path from arising. We can't endure in the development of morality, concentration and wisdom. It's just like that man sitting on the ants' nest. He can't do anything, the ants are biting and crawling all over him, he's immersed in confusion and agitation. He can't rid his sitting place of the danger, so he just sits there, suffering.

So it is with our practice. The worldly dhammas exist in the minds of worldly beings. When those beings wish to find peace the worldly dhammas arise right there. When the mind is ignorant there is only darkness. When knowledge arises the mind is illumined, because ignorance and knowledge are born in the same place. When ignorance has arisen, knowledge can't enter, because the mind has accepted ignorance. When knowledge has arisen, ignorance cannot stay.

So the Buddha exhorted his disciples to practise with the mind, because the world is born in this mind, the eight worldly dhammas are there. The Eightfold Path, that is, investigation through calm and insight meditation, our diligent effort and the wisdom we develop, all these things loosen the grip of the world. Attachment, aversion and delusion become lighter, and being lighter, we know them as such. If we experience fame, material gain, praise, happiness or suffering we're aware of it. We must know these things before we can transcend the world, because the world is within us.

When we're free of these things it's just like leaving a house. When we enter a house what sort of feeling do we have? We feel that we've come through the door and entered the house. When we leave the house we feel that we've left it, we come into the bright sunlight, it's not dark like it was inside. The action of the mind entering the worldly dhammas is like entering the house. The mind which has destroyed the worldly dhammas is like one who has left the house.

So the Dhamma practiser must become one who witnesses the Dhamma for himself. He knows for himself whether the worldly dhammas have left or not, whether or not the path has been developed. When the path has been well developed it purges the worldly dhammas. It becomes stronger and stronger. Right view grows as wrong view decreases, until finally the path destroys defilements - either that or defilements will destroy the path!

Right view and wrong view, there are only these two ways. Wrong view has its tricks as well, you know, it has its wisdom - but it's wisdom that's misguided. The meditator who begins to develop the path experiences a separation. Eventually it's as if he is two people - one in the world and the other on the path. They divide, they pull apart. Whenever he's investigating there's this separation, and it continues on and on until the mind reaches insight, vipassanā.

Or maybe it's *vipassanū!** Having tried to establish wholesome results in our practice, seeing them, we attach to them. This type of clinging comes from our wanting to get something from the practice. This is *vipassanū,* the wisdom of defilements (i.e. "defiled wisdom"). Some people develop goodness and cling to it, they develop purity and cling to that, or they develop knowledge and cling to that. The action of clinging to that goodness or knowledge is *vipassanū,* infiltrating our practice.

So when you develop *vipassanā,* be careful! Watch out for *vipassanū,* because they're so close that sometimes you can't tell them apart. But with right view we can see them both clearly. If it's *vipassanū* there will be suffering arising at times as a result. If it's really *vipassanā* there's no suffering. There is peace. Both happiness and unhappiness are silenced. This you can see for yourself.

This practice requires endurance. Some people, when they come to practise, don't want to be bothered by anything, they don't want friction. But there's friction the same as before. We must try to find an end to friction through friction itself! So, if there's friction in your practice, then it's right. If there's no friction it's not right, you just eat and sleep as much as you want. When you want to go anywhere or say anything you just follow your desires. The teaching of the Buddha

---

* ie. *Vipassanūpakkilesa* - the subtle defilements arising from meditation practice.

grates. The supermundane goes against the worldly. Right view opposes wrong view, purity opposes impurity. The teaching grates against our desires.

There's a story in the scriptures about the Buddha, before he was enlightened. At that time, having received a plate of rice, he floated that plate on a stream of water, determining in his mind, "If I am to be enlightened, may this plate float against the current of the water." The plate floated upstream! That plate was the Buddha's right view, or the Buddha-nature that he became awakened to. It didn't follow the desires of ordinary beings. It floated against the flow of his mind, it was contrary in every way.

These days, in the same way, the Buddha's teaching is contrary to our hearts. People want to indulge in greed and hatred but the Buddha won't let them. They want to be deluded but the Buddha destroys delusion. So the mind of the Buddha is contrary to that of worldly beings. The world calls the body beautiful, he says it's not beautiful. They say the body belongs to us, he says not so. They say it's substantial, he says it's not. Right view is above the world. Worldly beings merely follow the flow of the stream.

Continuing on, when the Buddha got up from there, he received eight handfuls of grass from a brahmin. The real meaning of this is that the eight handfuls of grass were the eight worldly dhammas-gain and loss, praise and criticism, fame and disrepute, happiness and unhappiness. The Buddha, having received this grass, determined to sit on it and enter *samādhi.* The action of sitting on the grass was itself *samādhi,* that is, his mind was above the worldly dhammas, subduing the world until it realized the transcendent. The worldly dhammas became like refuse for him, they lost all meaning. He sat over them but they didn't obstruct his mind in any way. The various māras came to try to overcome him, but he just sat there in *samādhi,* subduing the world, until finally he became enlightened to the Dhamma and completely defeated *Māra**. That is, he defeated the world. So the practice of developing the path is that which kills defilements.

People these days have little faith. Having practised a year or two they want to get there, and they want to go fast. They don't consider that the Buddha, our Teacher, had left home a full six years before he became enlightened. This is why we have *'freedom from dependence'.*** According to the scriptures, a monk must have at least five rains† before he is considered able to live on his own. By this time he has studied and practised sufficiently, he has adequate knowledge, he

---

* *Māra* (the Tempter), the Buddhist personification of evil. To the meditator it is all that obstructs the quest for enlightenment.

** 'Freedom from dependence' — A junior monk is expected to take 'dependence', that is, he lives under the guidance of a senior monk, for the first five years.

† 'rains' refers to the yearly three-month rains retreat by which monks count their age. Thus, a monk of five rains has been ordained for five years.

has faith, his conduct is good. Someone who practises for five years, I say he's competent. But he must really practise, not just *'hanging out'* in the robes for five years. He must really look after the practice, really do it!

Until you reach five rains you may wonder, "What is this *'freedom from dependence'* that the Buddha talked about?" You must really try to practise for five years and then you'll know for yourself the qualities he was referring to. After that time you should be competent, competent in mind, one who is certain. At the very least, after five rains, one should be at the first stage of enlightenment. This is not just five rains in body but five rains in mind as well. That monk has fear of blame, a sense of shame and modesty. He doesn't dare to do wrong either in front of people or behind their backs, in the light or in the dark. Why not? Because he has reached the Buddha, *'The One who knows'*. He takes refuge in the Buddha, the Dhamma and the Sangha.

To depend truly on the Buddha, the Dhamma and the Sangha we must see the Buddha. What use would it be to take refuge without knowing the Buddha? If we don't yet know the Buddha, the Dhamma and the Saṅgha, our taking refuge in them is just an act of body and speech, the mind still hasn't reached them. Once the mind reches them we know what the Buddha, the Dhamma and the Saṅgha are like. Then we can really take refuge in them, because these things arise in our minds. Wherever we are we will have the Buddha, the Dhamma and the Sangha with us.

One who is like this doesn't dare to commit evil acts. This is why we say that one who has reached the first stage of enlightenment will no longer be born in the woeful states. His mind is certain, he has entered the Stream, there is no doubt for him. If he doesn't reach full enlightenment today it will certainly be some time in the future. He may do wrong but not enough to send him to Hell, that is, he doesn't regress to evil bodily and verbal actions, he is incapable of it. So we say that person has entered the Noble Birth. He cannot return. This is something you should see and know for yourselves in this very life.

These days, those of us who still have doubts about the practice hear these things and say, "Oh, how can I do that?" Sometimes we feel happy, sometimes troubled, pleased or displeased. For what reason? Because we don't know Dhamma. What Dhamma? Just the Dhamma of Nature, the reality around us, the body and the mind.

The Buddha said, "Don't cling to the five *khandhas,* let them go, give them up!" Why can't we let them go? Just because we don't see them or know them fully. We see them as ourselves, we see ourselves in the *khandhas.* Happiness and suffering, we see as ourselves, we see ourselves in happiness and suffering. We can't separate ourselves from them. When we can't separate them it means we can't see Dhamma, we can't see Nature.

Happiness, unhappiness, pleasure and sadness - none of them is us but we take them to be so. These things come into contact with us and we see a lump of *'attā'*, or self. Wherever there is self there you will find happiness, unhappiness and everything else. So the Buddha said to destroy this *'lump'* of self, that is to destroy *sakkāya diṭṭhi.* When *attā* (self) is destroyed, *anattā* (non-self) naturally arises.

We take Nature to be us and ourselves to be Nature, so we don't know Nature truly. If it's good we laugh with it, if it's bad we cry over it. But Nature is simply sankhāras. As we say in the chanting, *'Tesam vūpasamo sukho'* - pacifying the *sankhāras* is real happiness. How do we pacify them? We simply remove clinging and see them as they really are.

So there is truth in this world. Trees, mountains and vines all live according to their own truth, they are born and die following their nature. It's just we people who aren't true! We see it and make a fuss over it, but Nature is impassive, it just is as it is. We laugh, we cry, we kill, but Nature remains in truth, it is truth. No matter how happy or sad we are, this body just follows its own nature. It's born, it grows up and ages, changing and getting older all the time. It follows Nature in this way. Whoever takes the body to be himself and carries it around with him, will suffer.

So *Aññā Kondañña* recognized this 'whatever is born' in everything, be it material or immaterial. His view of the world changed. He saw the truth. Having got up from his sitting place he took that truth with him. The activity of birth and death continued but he simply looked on. Happiness and unhappiness were arising and passing away but he merely noted them. His mind was constant. He no longer fell into the woeful states. He didn't get over-pleased or unduly upset about these things. His mind was firmly established in the activity of contemplation.

There! *Aññā Kondañña* had received the Eye of Dhamma. He saw Nature, which we call *sankhāras,* according to truth. Wisdom is that which knows the truth of *sankhāras.* This is the mind which knows and sees Dhamma, which has surrendered.

Until we have seen the Dhamma we must have patience and restraint. We must endure, we must renounce! We must cultivate diligence and endurance. Why must we cultivate diligence? Because we're lazy! Why must we develop endurance? Because we don't endure! That's the way it is. But when we are already established in our practice, have finished with laziness, then we don't need to use diligence. If we already know the truth of all mental states, if we don't get happy or unhappy over them, we don't need to exercise endurance, because the mind is already Dhamma. The 'one who knows' has seen the Dhamma, he is the Dhamma.

When the mind is Dhamma, it stops. It has attained peace. There's no longer a need to do anything special, because the mind is Dhamma already. The outside is Dhamma, the inside is Dhamma. The *'one who knows'* is Dhamma. The state is Dhamma and that which knows the state is Dhamma. It is one. It is free.

This Nature is not born, it does not age nor sicken. This Nature does not die. This Nature is neither happy nor sad, neither big nor small, heavy nor light; neither short nor long, black nor white. There's nothing you can compare it to. No convention can reach it. This is why we say *Nirvāna* has no colour. All colours are merely conventions. The state which is beyond the world is beyond the reach of worldly conventions.

So the Dhamma is that which is beyond the world. It is that which each person should see for himself. It is beyond language. You can't put it into words, you can only talk about ways and means of realizing it. The person who has seen it for himself has finished his work.

"...Regardless of time and place, the whole practice of Dhamma comes to completion at the place where there is nothing. It's the place of surrender, of emptiness, of laying down the burden..."

Convention and Liberation

The things of this world are merely conventions of our own making. Having established them we get lost in them, and refuse to let go, giving rise to clinging to our personal views and opinions. This clinging never ends, it is *saṁsāra,* flowing endlessly on. It has no completion. Now, if we know conventional reality then we'll know Liberation. If we clearly know Liberation, then we'll know convention. This is to know the Dhamma. Here there is completion.

Take people, for instance. In reality people don't have any names, we are simply born naked into the world. If we have names, they arise only through convention. I've contemplated this and seen that if you don't know the truth of this convention it can be really harmful. It's simply something we use for convenience. Without it we couldn't communicate, there would be nothing to say, no language.

I've seen the Westerners when they sit in meditation together in the West. When they get up after sitting, men and women together, sometimes they go and touch each other on the head!* When I saw this I thought, "Ehh, if we cling to convention it gives rise to defilements right there." If we can let go of convention, give up our opinions, we are at peace.

Like the generals and colonels, men of rank and position, who come to see me. When they come they say, "Oh, please touch my head."** If they ask like this there's nothing wrong with it, they're glad to have their heads touched. But if you tapped their heads in the middle of the street it'd be a different story! This is because of clinging. So I feel that letting go is really the way to peace. Touching a head is against our customs, but in reality it is nothing. When they agree to having it touched there's nothing wrong with it, just like touching a cabbage or a potato.

Accepting, giving up, letting go - this is the way of lightness. Wherever you're clinging there's becoming and birth right there. There's danger right there. The Buddha taught about convention and he taught to undo convention in the right way, and so reach Liberation.

---

* The head is regarded as sacred in Thailand, and to touch a person's head is considered an insult. Also, according to tradition, men and women do not touch each other in public. On the other hand, sitting in meditation is regarded as a 'holy' activity. Perhaps here the Venerable Ajahn was using an example of Western behaviour which would particularly shock his Thai audience.

** It is considered auspicious in Thailand to have one's head touched by a highly esteemed monk.

This is freedom, not to cling to conventions. All things in this world have a conventional reality. Having established them we should not be fooled by them,because getting lost in them really leads to suffering. This point concerning rules and conventions is of utmost importance. One who can get beyond them is beyond suffering.

However, they are a characteristic of our world. Take Mr. Boonmah, for instance; he used to be just one of the crowd but now he's been appointed the District Commissioner. It's just a convention but it's a convention we should respect. It's part of the world of people. If you think, "Oh, before we were friends, we used to work at the tailor's together," and then you go and pat him on the head in public, he'll get angry. It's not right, he'll resent it. So we should follow the conventions in order to avoid giving rise to resentment. It's useful to understand convention, living in the world is just about this. Know the right time and place, know the person.

Why is it wrong to go against conventions? It's wrong because of people! You should be clever, knowing both convention and Liberation. Know the right time for each. If we know how to use rules and conventions comfortably then we are skilled. But if we try to behave according to the higher level of reality in the wrong situation, this is wrong. Where is it wrong? It's wrong with people's defilements, nothing else! People all have defilements. In one situation we behave one way, in another situation we must behave in another way. We should know the ins and outs because we live within conventions. Problems occur because people cling to them. If we suppose something to be, then it is. It's there because we suppose it to be there. But if you look closely, in the absolute sense these things don't really exist.

As I have often said, before we were laymen and now we are monks. We lived within the convention of *'layman'* and now we live within the convention of *'monk'*. We are monks by convention, not monks through Liberation. In the beginning we establish conventions like this, but if a person merely ordains, this doesn't mean he overcomes defilements. If we take a handful of sand and agree to call it salt, does this make it salt? It is salt, but only in name, not in reality. You couldn't use it to cook with. It's only use is within the realm of that agreement, because there's really no salt there, only sand. It becomes salt only through our supposing it to be so.

This word 'Liberation' is itself just a convention, but it refers to that beyond conventions. Having achieved freedom, having reached liberation, we still have to use convention in order to refer to it as liberation. If we didn't have convention we couldn't communicate, so it does have its use.

For example, people have different names but they are all people just the same. If we didn't have names to differentiate between them, and we wanted to call out to somebody standing in a crowd, saying. "Hey, Person! Person!", that would be useless. You couldn't say who would answer you because they're all 'person'. But if you called, "Hey, John!", then John would come, the others wouldn't answer. Names fulfill just this need. Through them we can communicate, they provide the basis for social behaviour.

So you should know both convention and liberation. Conventions have a use, but in reality there really isn't anything there. Even people are non-existent! They are merely groups of elements, born of causal conditions, growing dependent on conditions, existing for a while, then disappearing in the natural way. No-one can oppose or control it. But without conventions we would have nothing to say, we'd have no names, no practice, no work. Rules and conventions are established to give us a language, to make things convenient, and that's all.

Take money, for example. In olden times there weren't any coins or notes, they had no value. People used to barter goods, but those things were difficult to keep, so they created money using coins and notes. Perhaps in the future we'll have a new king decree that we don't have to use paper money, we should use wax, melting it down and pressing it into lumps. We say this is money and use it throughout the country. Let alone wax, it may even happen that they decide to make chicken dung the local currency - all the other things can't be money, just chicken dung! Then people would fight and kill each otheer over chicken dung! This is the way it is. You could use many examples to illustrate convention. What we use for money is simply a convention that we have set up, it has its use within that convention. Having decreed it to be money, it becomes money. But in reality, what is money? Nobody can say. When there is a popular agreement about something, then a convention comes about to fulfill the need. The world is just this.

This is convention, but to get ordinary people to understand liberation is really difficult. Our money, our house, our family, our children and relatives are simply conventions that we have invented, but really, seen in the light of Dhamma, they don't belong to us. Maybe if we hear this we don't feel so good, but reality is like that. These things have value only through the established conventions. If we establish that it doesn't have value, then it doesn't have value. If we establish that it has value, then it has value. This is the way it is, we bring convention into the world to fulfill a need.

Even this body is not really ours, we just suppose it to be so. It's truly just a supposition. If you try to find a real, substantial self within it, you can't. There are merely elements which are born, continue for a while and then die. Everything is like this. There's no real, true substance to it, but it's proper that we use it. It's like a cup. At some time that cup must break, but while it's there you should use it and look after it well. It's a tool for your use. If it breaks there is trouble, so even though it must break, you should try your utmost to preserve it. And so we have the four supports* which

* The four supports-robes, alms-food, lodgings and medicines

the Buddha taught again and again to contemplate. They are the supports on which a monk depends to continue his practice. As long as you live you must depend on them, but you should understand them. Don't cling to them, giving rise to craving in your mind.

Convention and liberation are related like this continually. Even though we use convention, don't place your trust in it as being the truth. If you cling to it, suffering will arise. The case of right and wrong is a good example. Some people see wrong as being right and right as being wrong, but in the end who really knows what is right and what is wrong? We don't know. Different people establish different conventions about what's right and what's wrong, but the Buddha took suffering as his guide-line. If you want to argue about it there's no end to it. One says "right," another says "wrong". One says "wrong", another says "right." In truth we don't really know right and wrong at all! But at a useful, practical level, we can say that right is not to harm oneself and not to harm others. This way fulfills a use.

So, after all, both rules and conventions and liberation are simply dhammas. One is higher than the other, but they go hand in hand. There is no way that we can guarantee that anything is definitely like this or like that, so the Buddha said to just leave it be. Leave it be as uncertain. However much you like it or dislike it, you should understand it as uncertain.

Regardless of time and place, the whole practice of Dhamma comes to completion at the place where there is nothing. It's the place of surrender, of emptiness, of laying down the burden. This is the finish. It's not like the person who says, "Why is the flag fluttering in the wind? I say it's because of the wind." Another person says it's because of the flag. The other retorts that it's because of the wind. There's no end to this! The same as the old riddle, "Which came first, the chicken or the egg?" There's no way to reach a conclusion, this is just Nature.

All these things we say are merely conventions, we establish them ourselves. If you know these things with wisdom then you'll know impermanence, unsatisfactoriness and not-self. This is the outlook which leads to enlightenment.

You know, training and teaching people with varying levels of understanding is really difficult. Some people have certain ideas, you tell them something and they don't believe you. You tell them the truth and they say it's not true. "I'm right, you're wrong..." There's no end to this. If you don't let go there will be suffering. I've told you before about the four men who go into the forest. They hear a chicken crowing, "Kak-ka-dehhhh!" One of them wonders, "Is that a rooster or a hen?" Three of them say together, "It's a hen," but the other doesn't agree, he insists it's a rooster. "How could a hen crow like that?" he asks. They retort, "Well, it has a mouth, hasn't it?" They argue and argue till the tears fall, really getting upset over it, but in the end they're all wrong. Whether you say a hen or a rooster, they're only names. We establish these conventions, saying a rooster is like this, a hen is like that; a rooster cries like this, a hen cries like that ... and this is how we get stuck in the world! Remember this! Actually, if you just say that really there's no hen and no rooster then that's the end of it. In the field of conventional reality one side is right and the other side it wrong, but there will never be complete agreement. Arguing till the tears fall has no use!

The Buddha taught not to cling. How do we practise non-clinging? We practise simply to give up clinging, but this non-clinging is very difficult to understand. It takes keen wisdom to investigate and penetrate this, to really achieve non-clinging. When you think about it, whether people are happy or sad, content or discontent, doesn't depend on their having little or having much - it depends on wisdom. All distress can be transcended only through wisdom, through seeing the truth of things.

So the Buddha exhorted us to investigate, to contemplate. This *'contemplation'* means simply to try to solve these problems correctly. This is our practice. Like birth, old age, sickness and death - they are the most natural and common of occurences. The Buddha taught to contemplate birth, old age, sickness and death, but some people don't understand this. "What is there to contemplate?" they say. They're born but they don't know birth, they will die but they don't know death.

A person who investigates these things repeatedly will see. Having seen he will gradually solve his problems.

Even if he still has clinging, if he has wisdom and sees that old age, sickness and death are the way of Nature, then he will be able to relieve suffering. We study the Dhamma simply for this - to cure suffering. There isn't really much as the basis of Buddhism, there's just the birth and death of suffering, and this the Buddha called the truth. Birth is suffering, old age is suffering, sickness is suffering and death is suffering. People don't see this suffering as the truth. If we know truth, then we know suffering.

This pride in personal opinions, these arguments, they have no end. In order to put our minds at rest, to find peace, we should contemplate our past, the present, and the things which are in store for us. Like birth, old age, sickness and death. What can we do to avoid being plagued by these? Even though we may still have a little worry, if we investigate till we know according to the truth, all suffering will abate, we will no longer cling to it.

"...The worldly way is to do things for a reason, to get some return, but in Buddhism we do things without any gaining idea.. If we don't wan't anything at all, what will we get? We don't get anything! Whatever you get is just a cause for suffering, so we practise not getting anything... Just make the mind peaceful and have done with it!..."

No abiding

We hear some parts of the teachings and can't really understand them. We think they shouldn't be the way they are, so we don't follow them, but really there is a reason to all the teachings. Maybe it seems that things shouldn't be that way, but they are. At first I didn't even believe in sitting meditation. I couldn't see what use it would be to just sit with your eyes closed. And walking meditation...walk from this tree to that tree, turn around and walk back again... "Why bother?" I thought, "What's the use of all that walking?" I thought like that, but actually walking and sitting meditation are of great use.

Some people's tendencies make them prefer walking meditation, others prefer sitting, but you can't do without either of them. In the scriptures they talk about the four postures: standing, walking, sitting and lying. We live with these four postures. We may prefer one to the other, but we must use all four.

They say to make these four postures even, to make the practice even in all postures. At first I couldn't figure out what this meant, to make them even. Maybe it means we sleep for two hours, then stand for two hours, then walk for two hours...maybe that's it? I tried it -

couldn't do it, it was impossible! That's not what it meant to make the postures even. 'Making the postures even' refers to the mind, to our awareness. That is, to make the mind give rise to wisdom, to illumine the mind. This wisdom of ours must be present in all postures; we must know, or understand, constantly. Standing, walking, sitting or lying, we know all mental states as impermanent, unsatisfactory and not-self. Making the postures even in this way can be done, it is possible. Whether like or dislike are present in the mind we don't forget our practice, we are aware.

If we just focus our attention on the mind constantly then we have the gist of the practice. Whether we experience mental states which the world knows as good or bad we don't forget ourselves, we don't get lost in good or bad. We just go straight. Making the postures constant in this way is possible. If we have constancy in our practice and we are praised, then it's simply praise; if we are blamed, then it's just blame. We don't get high or low over it, we stay right here. Why? Because we see the danger in all those things, we see their results. We are constantly aware of the danger in both praise and blame. Normally, if we have a good mood the mind is good also, we see them as the same thing; if we have a bad mood the mind goes bad as well, we don't like it. This is the way it is, this is uneven practice.

If we have constancy just to the extent of knowing our moods, and knowing we're clinging to them, this is better already. That is, we have awareness, we know what's going on, but we still can't let go. We see ourselves clinging to good and bad, and we know it. We cling to good and know it's still not right practice, but we still can't let go. This is 50% or 70% of the practice already. There still isn't release but we know that if we could let go that would be the way to peace. We keep going like that, seeing the equally harmful consequences of all our likes and dislikes, of praise and blame, continuously. Whatever there is, the mind is constant in this way.

But for worldly people, if they get blamed or criticized they get really upset. If they get praised it cheers them up, they say it's good and get really happy over it. If we know the truth of our various moods, if we know the consequences of clinging to praise and blame, the danger of clinging to anything at all, we will become sensitive to our moods. We will know that clinging to them really causes suffering. We see this suffering, and we see our very clinging as the cause of that suffering. We begin to see the consequences of grabbing and clinging to good and bad, because we've grasped them and seen the result before - no real happiness. So now we look for the way to let go.

Where is this 'way to let go'? In Buddhism we say "Don't cling to anything." We never stop hearing about this "don't cling to anything!" This means to hold, but not to cling. Like this flashlight. We think, "What is this?" So we pick it up, "Oh, it's a flashlight," then we put it down again. We hold things in this way. If we didn't hold anything at all, what could we do?

We couldn't walk meditation or do anything, so we must hold things first. It's wanting, yes, that's true, but later on it leads to *'parami'* (virtue or perfection). Like wanting to come here, for instance... *Venerable Jāgaro* * came to Wat Pah Pong. He had to want to come first. If he hadn't felt that he wanted to come he wouldn't have come. For anybody it's the same, they come here because of wanting. But when wanting arises don't cling to it! So you come, and then you go back... What is this? We pick it up, look at it and see, "Oh, it's a flashlight," then we put it down. This is called holding but not clinging, we let go. We know and then we let go. To put it simply we say just this, "Know, then let go." Keep looking and letting go. "This, they say is good; this, they say is not good"...know, and then let go. Good and bad, we know it all, but we let it go. We don't foolishly cling to things, but we *'hold'* them with wisdom. Practising in this *'posture'* can be constant. You must be constant like this. Make the mind know in this way, let wisdom arise. When the mind has wisdom, what else is there to look for?

We should reflect on what we are doing here. For what reason are we living here, what are we working for? In the world they work for this or that reward, but the monks teach something a little deeper than that. Whatever we do, we ask for no return. We work for no reward. Worldly people work because they want

---

* *Venerble Jāgaro* the Australian Abbot of Wat Pah Nanachat at that time, who brought his party of monks and laypeople to see Ajahn Chah.

this or that, because they want some gain or other, but the Buddha taught to work just in order to work, we don't ask for anything beyond that. If you do something just to get some return it'll cause suffering. Try it out for yourself! You want to make your mind peaceful so you sit down and try to make it peaceful - you'll suffer! Try it. Our way is more refined. We do, and then let go; do, and then let go.

Look at the brahmin who makes a sacrifice: he has some desire in mind, so he makes a sacrifice. Those actions of his won't help him transcend suffering because he's acting on desire. In the beginning we practise with some desire in mind; we practise on and on, but we don't attain our desire. So we practise until we reach a point where we're practising for no return, we're practising in order to let go. This is something we must see for ourselves, it's very deep. Maybe we practise because we want to go to *Nirvāna* - right there, you won't get to *Nirvāna!* It's natural to want peace, but it's not really correct. We must practise without wanting anything at all. If we don't want anything at all, what will we get? We don't get anything! Whatever you get is just a cause for suffering, so we practise not getting anything.

Just this is called *'making the mind empty'*. It's empty but there is still doing. This emptiness is something people don't usually understand, but those who reach it see the value of knowing it. It's not the emptiness of not having anything, it's emptiness within the things that are here. Like this flashlight: we should see this flashlight as empty, because of the flashlight there is emptiness. It's not the emptiness where we can't see anything, it's not like that. People who understand like that have got it all wrong. You must understand emptiness within the things the are here.

Those who are still practising because of some gaining idea are like the brahmin who makes a sacrifice just to fulfill some wish. Like the people who come to see me to be sprinkled with 'holy water'. When I ask them, "Why do you want this 'holy water?" they say, "We want to live happily and comfortably and not get sick." There! They'll never transcend suffering that way. The worldly way is to do things for a reason, to get some return, but in Buddhism we do things without any gaining idea. The world has to understand things in terms of cause and effect, but the Buddha teaches us to go above and beyond cause and effect. His wisdom was to go above cause, beyond effect; to go above birth and beyond death; to go above happiness and beyond suffering. Think about it...there's nowhere to stay. We people live in a 'home'. To leave home and go where there is no home ...we don't know how to do it, because we've always lived with becoming , with clinging. If we can't cling we don't know what to do.

So most people don't want to go to *Nirvāna,* there's nothing there; nothing at all. Look at the roof and the floor here. The upper extreme is the roof, that's an *"abiding".* The lower extreme is the floor, and that's another *"abiding"*. But in the empty space between the floor and the roof there's nowhere stand. One could stand on the roof, or stand on the floor, but not on that empty space. Where there is no abiding, that's where there's emptiness, and, to put it bluntly, we say that *Nirvāna* is this emptiness. People hear this and they back up a bit, they don't want to go. They're afraid they won't see their children or relatives.

This is why, when we bless the laypeople, we say "May you have long life, beauty, happiness and strength." This makes them really happy, *"Sādhu!"** they all say. They like these things. If you start talking about emptiness they don't want it, they're attached to abiding. But have you ever seen a very old person with a beautiful complexion? Have you ever seen an old person with a lot of strength, or a lot of happiness? ...No... But we say, "Long life, beauty, happiness and strength" and they're all really pleased, every single one says "Sādhu!" This is like the brahmin who makes oblations to achieve some wish. In our practice we don't *'make oblations'*, we don't practise in order to get some return. We don't want anything. If we still want something then there is still something there. Just make the mind peaceful and have done with it! But if I talk like this you may not be very comfortable, because you want to be 'born' again.

So all you lay practisers should get close to the monks and see their practice. To be close to the monks means to be close to the Buddha, to be close to his

* *"Sādhu"* is the traditional Pāli word used to acknowledge a blessing, dhamma teaching, etc. It means "it is well."

Dhamma. The Buddha said, "*Ānanda,* practise a lot, develop your practice! Whoever sees the Dhamma sees me, and whoever sees me sees the Dhamma." Where is the Buddha? We may think the Buddha has been and gone, but the Buddha is the Dhamma, the Truth. Some people like to say, "Oh, if I was born in the time of the Buddha I would go to *Nirvāna.*" Here, stupid people talk like this. The Buddha is still here. The Buddha is truth. Regardless of whoever is born or dies, the truth is still here. The truth never departs from the world, it's there all the time. Whether a Buddha is born or not, whether someone knows it or not, the truth is still there. So we should get close to the Buddha, we should come within and find the Dhamma. When we reach the Dhamma we will reach the Buddha; seeing the Dhamma we will see the Buddha and all doubts will dissolve.

To put it simply, it's like Teacher Choo.* At first he wasn't a teacher, he was just Mr. Choo. When he studied and passed the necessary grades he became a teacher, and became known as Teacher Choo. How did he become a teacher? Through studying the required things, thus allowing Mr. Choo to become Teacher Choo. When Teacher Choo dies, the study to become a teacher still remains, and whoever studies it will become

---

* In Thailand the word 'Teacher' is used as a title of address much like 'Doctor' is used in English. 'Teacher Choo' is one of four elderly local residents who came to spend the rains retreat at Wat Pah Nanachat, to whom the latter part of this talk was addressed.

a teacher. That course of study to become a teacher doesn't disappear anywhere, just like the Truth, the knowing of which enabled the Buddha to become the Buddha. So the Buddha is still here. Whoever practises and sees the Dhamma sees the Buddha. These days people have got it all wrong, they don't know where the Buddha is. They say, "If I was born in the time of the Buddha I would have become a disciple of his and become enlightened." That's just foolishness. You should understand this.

Don't go thinking that at the end of the rains retreat you'll disrobe. Don't think like that! In an instant an evil thought can arise in the mind, you could kill somebody. In the same way, it only takes a split-second for good to flash into the mind, and you're there already. Don't think that you have to ordain for a long time to be able to meditate. Where the right practice lies is in the instant we make kamma. In a flash an evil thought arises... before you know it you've committed some really heavy kamma. And in the same way, all the disciples of the Buddha practised for a long time, but the time they attained enlightenment was merely one thought moment. So don't be heedless, even in minor things. Try hard, try to get close to the monks, contemplate things and then you'll know about monks. Well, that's enough, huh? It must be getting late now, some people are getting sleepy. The Buddha said not to teach Dhamma to sleepy people.

"...Our discontent is due to wrong view. Because we don't exercise sense restraint we blame our suffering on externals... The right abiding place for monks, the place of coolness, is just Right View itself. We shouldn't look for anything else..."

Right view-The place of coolness

The practice of Dhamma goes against our habits, the truth goes against our desires, so there is difficulty in the practice. Some things which we understand as wrong may be right, while the things we take to be right may be wrong. Why is this? Because our minds are in darkness, we don't clearly see the Truth. We don't really know anything and so are fooled by people's lies. They point out what is right as being wrong and we believe it; that which is wrong, they say is right, and we believe that. This is because we are not yet our own masters. Our moods lie to us constantly. We shouldn't take this mind and its opinions as our guide, because it doesn't know the truth.

Some people don't want to listen to others at all, but this is not the way of a man of wisdom. A wise man listens to everything. One who listens to Dhamma must listen just the same, whether he likes it or not, and not blindly believe or disbelieve. He must stay at the half-way mark, the middle point, and not be heedless. He just listens and then contemplates, giving rise to the right results accordingly.

A wise man should contemplate and see the cause and effect for himself before he believes what he hears.

Even if the teacher speaks the truth, don't just believe it, because you don't yet know the truth of it for yourself.

It's the same for all of us, including myself. I've practised before you, I've seen many lies before. For instance, "This practice is really difficult, really hard." Why is the practice difficult? It's just because we think wrongly, we have wrong view.

Previously I lived together with other monks, but I didn't feel right. I ran away to the forests and mountains, fleeing the crowd, the monks and novices. I thought that they weren't like me, they didn't practise as hard as I did. They were sloppy. That person was like this, this person was like that. This was something that really put me in turmoil, it was the cause for my continually running away. But whether I lived alone or with others I still had no peace. On my own I wasn't content, in a large group I wasn't content. I thought this discontent was due to my companions, due to my moods, due to my living place, the food, the weather, due to this and that. I was constantly searching for something to suit my mind.

As a *dhutanga** monk, I went travelling, but things still weren't right. So I contemplated, "What can I do

---

* *Dhutanga,* properly means *'ascetic'*. A Dhutanga monk is one who keeps some of the thirteen ascetic practices allowed by the Buddha. Dhutanga monks traditionally spend time travelling (often on foot) in search of quiet places for meditation, other teachers, or simply as a practice in itself.

to make things right? What can I do?'' Living with a lot of people I was dissatisfied, with few people I was dissatisfied. For what reason? I just couldn't see it. Why was I dissatisfied? Because I had wrong view, just that; because I still clung to the wrong Dhamma. Wherever I went I was discontent, thinking, ''Here is no good, there is no good...'' on and on like that. I blamed others. I blamed the weather, heat and cold, I blamed everything! Just like a mad dog. It bites whatever it meets, because it's mad. When the mind is like this our practice is never settled. Today we feel good, tomorrow no good. It's like that all the time. We don't attain contentment or peace.

The Buddha once saw a jackal, a wild dog, run out of the forest where he was staying. It stood still for a while, then it ran into the underbrush, and then out again. Then it ran into a tree hollow, then out again. Then it went into a cave, only to run out again. One minute it stood, the next it ran, then it lay down, then it jumped up..That jackal had mange. When it stood the mange would eat into its skin, so it would run. Running it was still uncomfortable, so it would stop. Standing was still uncomfortable, so it would lie down. Then it would jump up again, running into the underbrush, the tree hollow, never staying still.

The Buddha said, ''Monks, did you see that jackal this afternoon? Standing it suffered, running it suffered, sitting it suffered, lying down it suffered. In the underbrush, a tree hollow or a cave, it suffered. It blamed standing for its discomfort, it blamed sitting, it blamed running and lying down; it blamed the tree, the underbrush and the cave. In fact the problem was with none of those things. That jackal had mange. The problem was with the mange.''

We monks are just the same as that jackal. Our discontent is due to wrong view. Because we don't exercise sense restraint we blame our suffering on externals. Whether we live at Wat Pah Pong, in America or in London we aren't satisfied. Going to live at Bung Wai or any of the other branch monasteries we're still not satisfied. Why not? Because we still have wrong view within us, just that! Wherever we go we aren't content.

But just as that dog, if the mange is cured, is content wherever it goes, so it is for us. I reflect on this often, and I teach you this often, because it's very important. If we know the truth of our various moods we arrive at contentment. Whether it's hot or cold we are satisfied, with many people or with few people we are satisfied. Contentment doesn't depend on how many people we are with, it comes only from right view. If we have right view then wherever we stay we are content.

But most of us have wrong view. It's just like a maggot! A maggot's living place is filthy, its food is filthy...but they suit the maggot. If you take a stick and brush it away from its lump of dung, it'll struggle to crawl back into it. It's the same when the Ajahn teaches us to see rightly. We resist, it makes us feel uneasy. We run back to our *'lump of dung'* because that's where we feel at home. We're all like this. If we don't see the harmful consequences of all our wrong views then we can't leave them, the practice is difficult. So we should listen. There's nothing else to the practice.

If we have right view wherever we go we are content. I have practised and seen this already. These days there are many monks, novices and laypeople coming to see me. If I still didn't know, if I still had wrong view, I'd be dead by now! The right abiding place for monks, the place of coolness, is just right view itself. We shouldn't look for anything else.

So even though you may be unhappy it doesn't matter, that unhappiness is uncertain. Is that unhappiness your *'self'?* Is there any substance to it? Is it real? I don't see it as being real at all. Unhappiness is merely a flash of feeling which appears and then is gone. Happiness is the same. Is there a consistency to happiness? Is it truly an entity? It's simply a feeling that flashes suddenly and is gone. There! It's born and then it dies. Love just flashes up for a moment and then disappears. Where is the consistency in love, or hate, or resentment? In truth there is no substantial entity there, they are merely impressions which flare up in the mind and then die. They deceive us constantly, we find no certainty anywhere. Just as the Buddha said, when unhappiness arises it stays for a while, then disappears. When unhappiness disappears, happiness arises and lingers for a while and then dies. When happiness disappears, unhappiness arises again... on and on like this.

In the end we can say only this - apart from the birth, the life and the death of Suffering, there is nothing. There is just this. But we who are ignorant run and grab it constantly. We never see the truth of it, that there's simply this continual change. If we understand this then we don't need to think very much, but we have much wisdom. If we don't know it, then we will have more thinking than wisdom - and maybe no wisdom at all! It's not until we truly see the harmful results of our actions that we can give them up. Likewise, it's not until we see the real benefits of practice that we can follow it, and begin working to make the mind *'good'*.

If we cut a log of wood and throw it into the river, and that log doesn't sink or rot, or run aground on either of the banks of the river, that log will definitely reach the sea. Our practice is comparable to this. If you practise according to the path laid down by the Buddha, following it straightly, you will transcend two things. What two things? Just those two extremes that the Buddha said were not the path of a true meditator - Indulgence in pleasure and indulgence in pain. These are the two banks of the river. One of the banks of that river is hate, the other is love. Or you can say that one bank is happiness, the other unhappiness. The *'log'* is this mind. As it *'flows down the river'* it will experience happiness and unhappiness. If the mind doesn't cling to that happiness or unhappiness it will reach the *'ocean'* of *Nirvāna.* You should see that there is nothing other than happiness and unhappiness arising and disappearing. If you don't *'run aground'* on these things then you are on the path of a true meditator.

This is the teaching of the Buddha. Happiness, unhappiness, love and hate are simply established in Nature according to the constant law of nature. The wise person doesn't follow or encourage them, he doesn't cling to them. This is the mind which lets go of indulgence in pleasure and indulgence in pain. It is the right practice. Just as that log of wood will eventually flow to the sea, so will the mind which doesn't attach to these two extremes inevitably attain peace.

Epilogue

...Do you know where it will end? Or will you just keep on learning like this? ...Or is there an end to it?... That's okay but it's the external study, not the internal study. For the internal study you have to study these eyes, these ears, this nose, this tongue, this body and this mind. This is the real study. The study of books is just the external study, it's really hard to get it finished.

When the eye sees form what sort of thing happens? When ear, nose and tongue experience sounds, smells and tastes, what takes place? When the body and mind come into contact with touches and mental states, what reactions take place? Are there still greed, aversion and delusion there? Do we get lost in forms, sounds, smells, tastes, textures and moods? This is the internal study. It has a point of completion.

If we study but don't practise we won't get any results. It's like a person who raises cows. In the morning he takes the cow out to eat grass, in the evening he brings it back to its pen - but he never drinks the cow's milk. Study is alright, but don't let it be like this. You should raise the cow and drink its milk too. You must study and practise as well to get the best results.

Here, I'll explain it further. It's like a person who raises chickens, but he doesn't get the eggs. All he gets is the chicken dung! This is what I tell the people who raise chickens back home! Watch out you don't become like that! This means we study the scriptures but we don't know how to let go of defilements, we don't know how to *'push'* greed, aversion and delusion from our mind. Study without practice, without this *'giving up'*, brings no results. This is why I compare it to someone who raises chickens but doesn't collect the eggs, he just collects the dung. It's the same thing.

Because of this, the Buddha wanted us to study the scriptures, and then to give up evil actions through body, speech and mind; to develop goodness in our deeds, speech and thoughts. The real worth of mankind will come to fruition through our deeds, speech and thoughts. But if we only talk well, without acting accordingly, it's not yet complete. Or if we do good deeds but the mind is still not good, this is still not complete. The Buddha taught to develop goodness in body, speech and mind; to develop fine deeds, fine speech and fine thoughts. This is the treasure of mankind. The study and the practice must both be good.

The Eightfold Path of the Buddha, the path of practice, has eight factors. These eight factors are nothing other than this very body: two eyes, two ears, two nostrils, one tongue and one body. This is the path. And the mind is the one who follows the path. Therefore both the study and the practice exist in our body, speech and mind.

Epilogue

Have you ever seen scriptures which teach about anything other than the body, the speech and the mind? The scriptures only teach about this; nothing else. Defilements are born right here. If you know them they die right here. So you should understand that the practice and the study both exist right here. If we study just this much we can know everything. It's like our speech: to speak one word of Truth is better than a lifetime of wrong speech. Do you understand? One who studies and doesn't practise is like a ladle in a soup pot. It's in the pot every day but it doesn't know the flavour of the soup. If you don't practice, even if you study till the day you die, you won't know *the taste of Freedom!*

Note on selected talks

1. **On meditation**—an informal talk given in the Northeastern dialect, taken from an unidentified tape.
2. **The path in harmony**—a composite of two talks given in England in 1979 and 1977 respectively.
3. **The middle way within**—given in the Northeastern dialect to an assembly of monks and laypeople in 1970
4. **The peace beyond**—a condensed version of a talk given to the Chief Privy Councillor of Thailand, Mr. Sanya Dharmasakti, at wat Nong Pah Pong, 1978
5. **Opening the dhamma eye**—given at wat Nong Pah Pong to the assembly of monks and novices in October, 1968.
6. **Convention and Liberation**—an informal talk given in the Northeastern dialect, taken from an identified tape.
7. **No abiding**—a talk given to the monks, novices and laypeople of Wat Pah Nanachat on a visit to Wat Nong Pah Pong during the rains of 1980.

Venerable Ajahn Chah *(Pra Bhodinyāna Thera)* was born into a typical farming family in Bahn Gor village, in the province of Ubol Rachathani, N.E. Thailand, in 1917. He lived the first part of his life as any other youngster in rural Thailand, and, following the custom, took ordination as a novice in the local village *Wat* for a number of years, where he learned to read and write, in addition to some basic Buddhist teachings. After a number of years he returned to the lay life to help his parents, but, feeling an attraction to the monastic life, at the age of twenty he again entered a *Wat,* this time for higher ordination as a *bhikkhu,* or Buddhist monk.

He spent the first few years of his *bhikkhu* life studying scriptures and learning Pali, but the death of his father awakened him to the transience of life and instilled in him a desire to find the real essence of the Buddha's teaching. He began to travel to other monasteries, studying the monastic discipline in detail and spending a very brief but significant time with **Venerable Ajahn Mun,** the most outstanding meditation Master of the ascetic, forest – dwelling tradition. Following his time with Venerable Ajahn Mun, he spent a number of years travelling around Thailand, spending his time in forests and charnel grounds, ideal places for developing meditation practice.

At length he came within the vicinity of the village of his birth, and when word got around that he was in the area, he was invited to set up a monastery at the *Pa Pong* forest, a place at that time reputed to be the habitat of wild animals and ghosts. Venerable Ajahn Chah's impeccable approach to meditation, or *Dhamma* practice, and his simple, direct style of teaching, with the emphasis on practical application and a balanced attitude, began to attract a large following of monks and laypeople.

In 1966 the first westerner came to stay at *Wat Pa Pong,* **Venerable Sumedho Bhikkhu.** From that time on, the number of foreign people who came to Ajahn Chah began to steadily increase, until in 1975, the first branch monastery for western and other non-Thai nationals, *Wat Pa Nanachat,* was set up with Venerable Ajahn Sumedho as the abbot.

The 1976 Venerable Ajahn Chah was invited to England together with Ajahn Sumedho, the outcome of which was eventually the establishment of the first branch monastery of Wat Pa Pong outside of Thailand. Since then, further branch monasteries have been established in England, Switzerland, Australia, New Zealand and Italy.

In 1980 Venerable Ajahn Chah began to feel more accutely the symptoms of dizziness and memory lapse which he had been feeling for some years. This led to an operation in 1981, which, however, failed to reverse the onset of the paralysis which eventually rendered him completely bedridden and unable to speak. However this did not stop the growth of monks and laypeople who came to practise at his monastery, for whom the teachings of Ajahn Chah are a constant guide and inspiration.